YO-EGI-198

Mortal City

Peter Lang, editor

Princeton Architectural Press, New York
StoreFront Books 1

Published by
Princeton Architectural Press
37 East 7th Street
New York, New York 10003
212.995.9620
For a free catalog of books, call 1.800.458.1131.

Princeton Architectural Press
Design and editing: Clare Jacobson
Special thanks to Seonaidh Davenport, Caroline Green, Sarah
Lappin, Bill Monaghan, Allison Saltzman, and Ann C. Urban
—Kevin C. Lippert, publisher

 Mortal City is the first publication of Store-
Front Books, a project of StoreFront for Art
and Architecture, New York. Kyong Park is
editor and Tam Miller is associate editor.

Library of Congress Cataloging-in-Publication Data
Mortal city / edited by Peter Lang.
  p. cm. — (StoreFront books ; 1)
  Includes bibliographical references.
  ISBN 1-56898-046-9 (pbk.)
  1. Violence. 2. Cities and towns. I. Lang, Peter, 1957- .
II. Series.
HM281.M66 1995
303.6—dc20   95-867
                  CIP

Photo Credits
Cover: Ted Morrison, 1993
4: Peter Lang, 1994
8: Revere Copper and Brass Company, ca. 1943
12, 13: courtesy Senior Trademark Council, 1942–43
15: courtesy American Gas Association, 1943
18, 22, 23: Camilo José Vergara, 1988–92
36, 40–46, 54, 111: Warchitecture, 1994
69: Robin Evans. ©Janet Evans; used with permission
70, 102, 108: Stephane Herzog, 1993
82: Peter Anders, 1994

Contents

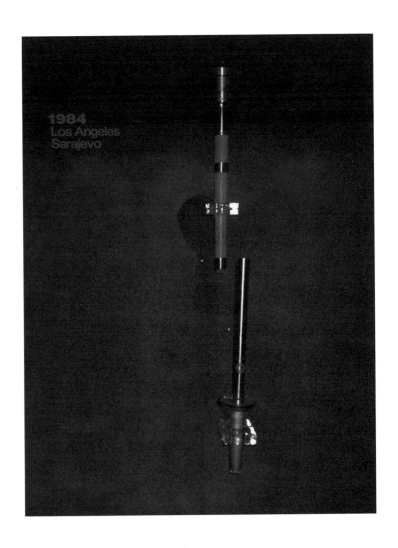

1984
Los Angeles
Sarajevo

Introduction
Peter Lang

During the cold war, the Soviets continuously altered their maps
so that cities would be hard to find. It was common knowledge
at the time that the most reliable street map of Moscow was at
CIA Headquarters. The city's real intersections were intention-
ally lost.

Cities are still being displaced, but no longer for tactical reasons. There are some postmodernists hard at work shifting the
city into the abstract realms of their theoretical landscapes. If the
Soviets demonstrated a lack of cartographic honesty, it was in
part justified by the precision of the American nuclear arsenal.
In the postmodern perspective, the city of real time and space is
still lost, precisely through lack of critical attention. *Mortal City*
aims to recover the city from the ground up.

Cities are susceptible to the inconsistencies of human rela-
tions, which are too often propelled by ambiguous notions of
blood, soil, family, and clan. Economic disparities and political
struggles also weaken urban societies. And cities defy with great
risk the extreme forces of nature. All too frequently the city's
survival hangs in a precious balance. The essays and documents
collected in *Mortal City* are engaged responses to the uncertain
future of the living city.

Few cities in the recent past have so forcefully occupied
international attention as Sarajevo and Los Angeles. They have

Torches from the 1984 Olympic Games, Olympic Museum, Lausanne, Switzerland become infamous for their experiences in social and political destabilization. But their human struggles, so intimately presented to a world audience, nonetheless appear inaccessible and incomprehensible. Sarajevo and Los Angeles represent two unsettling examples of cities caught in protracted urban crises. They have served, from the start, to structure the working parameters of this project.

There exists, however, a historical twist to this paradigm. Sarajevo and Los Angeles were, a decade ago, upheld as model cities; in the Orwellian year of 1984, both were honored hosts to Olympic Games. These competitions took place in the heightened atmosphere of a Soviet boycott and under the backdrop of nationalistic rivalry. But significantly, both the Winter Games in Sarajevo and the Summer Games in Los Angeles were free from incidents of violence like those that shook Mexico city in 1968 and paralyzed Munich in 1972. In 1984 Sarajevo and Los Angeles reveled in Olympic ceremony.

But athletic competitions are short lived. Like their *Potemkin* predecessors, the Olympic villages left few enduring traces. The cosmetic flurry of housecleaning, banner hanging, and surgical measures performed on the urban infrastructures only temporarily enhanced each city's international prestige. The memory of these two cities as model hosts faded quickly.

During the final days of April 1992, heavy fighting broke out in areas of what was then Yugoslavia. By the time Serbia and Montenegro announced the formation of a new Yugoslav state on the 27th of the month, the civil war around Sarajevo had settled into its pattern of destruction. Meanwhile, in Los Angeles, severe rioting erupted on April 29 after three white policemen were acquitted of the beating of Rodney King, a black citizen of the inner city.

Sarajevo and Los Angeles are gradually wasting away. Each new conflagration pushes at the limits of the humanly tolerable. In these increasingly hardened landscapes, city residents are forced to bunker down. For those who live in the valley of Sarajevo or in South-Central Los Angeles, the possibility of going about daily life has become exceedingly difficult. Exodus has become one of their few remaining options. They may rightly wonder if they have been unceremoniously abandoned.

The disparate voices and perspectives collected in *Mortal City* share a common concern for the threatened survival of urban society. It may be somewhat reassuring to note that the citizens of Sarajevo and Los Angeles are by no means broken; if anything, their spirits have strengthened considerably. It is to the daily struggle of the people of these two cities that *Mortal City* is dedicated.

Peter Lang is an architect and historian.

"After total war
can come total living"

World War II and the American Dream

Donald Albrecht

A young couple gazes confidently toward the bright, blissful horizon in a 1940's brochure for the Revere Copper and Brass Company. Above them floats the ominously thrilling message, "After Total War Can Come Total Living." This violent juxtaposition of text and image, like so much media produced during World War II, suggests a profound and transforming irony: while America remained physically untouched by the war's destruction, life in America was wedded to its specter.

From the fall of France in the summer of 1940 to V-J Day in August 1945, more than 17 million Americans, or fourteen percent of the population, served in the armed forces of World War II. More than 400,000 lost their lives; almost 700,000 were wounded. Yet for millions of Americans at home, a booming wartime economy produced a remarkable prosperity that ended the Great Depression, sparked a postwar economic miracle, and made the American Dream of suburban homes, shopping centers, and modern kitchens a reality.

In 1934 social and architectural historian Lewis Mumford wrote, "War is the health of the machine." Mumford's assertion was borne out by World War II, the first truly mechanized war in history. After instituting the first peacetime draft in 1940, the American government funded a massive building program that facilitated the nation's largest military mobilization. In less than

This illustration appeared in one of a series of brochures published during the war by the Revere Copper and Brass Company, manufacturers of household items such as pots and pans. Entitled "Revere's Part in Better Living," the series offered the public new concepts of postwar housing.

a year, army camp capacity quadrupled through the rapid construction of standardized barracks, mess halls, and other structures. These simple buildings captured a wartime ethos of con-
formity and consensus that later proved valuable to many who
traded their army fatigues for gray flannel suits. The same spirit of functional consequence gripped every facet of wartime construction, from the steady stream of the more than 170,000
American-made Quonset huts that were shipped overseas, to the
network of coastal defenses that guarded U.S. shores against
possible enemy attack. At the same time, the nation's industri-
alists, driven by patriotism and profit, entered into lucrative
partnerships with the federal government. Titans like Henry
Ford and Henry J. Kaiser revved up America's prewar consumer
economy into a hyperactive wartime engine. They converted,
expanded, and built thousands of factories, and produced un-
heard-of numbers of bombs, guns, ships, and tanks. By 1944,
aircraft capacity was twenty times what it had been in 1940, and
annual output was over 95,000 planes. In all, the government
invested 23 billion dollars in defense-related facilities. America's
productive capacity increased a staggering 15% per year from
1940 to 1944, while successful war bond campaigns and the
scarcity of consumer goods caused the savings rate to climb,
putting wealth in people's postwar pockets.

By many accounts, 1943 was the pivotal year in this remarkable story. A little more than a year after the humiliation of Pearl
Harbor, American forces captured Guadalcanal and began their
island-hopping campaign to regain Japanese-controlled bases in
the Pacific. The Allies invaded Sicily, the Germans surrendered
to the Russians at Stalingrad, and the Teheran Conference
launched plans for the Allied invasion of Normandy. At home,
the Pentagon was completed, and Americans learned of great,
morale-boosting production increases. Ford's Willow Run bomber plant outside Detroit increased production from 31 planes in
January to 190 in June. By January 1944, the company was
building more B-24s than anyone else, and by March an airplane rolled off the assembly line almost every hour. Willow
Run, Charles Lindbergh reportedly proclaimed, is "a Grand
Canyon of the mechanized world."[1]

At selected sites throughout the country, change was transforming the landscape. The city of Vanport, Oregon, a new town

of 40,000 people built to service Kaiser shipyards, was completed in 1943. Vanport illustrates the massive wartime migration of 15 million Americans in search of well-paid work at blossoming defense centers. The West Coast, with its vast aircraft and shipbuilding industries, witnessed the most remarkable change. From 1940 to 1947, the combined populations of California, Washington, and Oregon increased by nearly forty percent. Between 1940 and 1944, over 500,000 people moved to the Los Angeles area alone, while the population of San Diego increased by nearly fifty percent. This migration resulted in economic and demographic shifts that permanently altered the nation's regional balance, giving the West Coast newfound status and independence.

With victory almost in sight, the country shifted its attention to peacetime conversion. Congress passed the GI Bill of Rights to ease the return to civilian life. While austerity and material shortages were still in effect, manufacturers of prewar goods kept their names before the public eye by publicizing the wonders awaiting veterans. Magazines, unable to publish stories of top-secret military developments, speculated on life after the war. The dream house was promoted as central to postwar material comfort. This certainly was the hope of the Libbey-Owens-Ford Glass Company, whose model "kitchen of tomorrow" was covered by *Better Homes and Gardens* in July 1943 and later toured department stores across the nation. However, if the public longed for the day after war, they found the day before equally alluring, as evidenced by the popularity of Rogers and Hammerstein's *Oklahoma*, which premiered on Broadway during the same year.

The surge in home building brought on by wartime migration gave impetus to America's century-old interest in prefabricated housing. Architects, engineers, and manufacturers responded by inventing unusual residential schemes: "bubble" houses constructed by spraying concrete over inflated rubber forms, "stressed skin" construction that echoed advances in the aircraft industry, and even dwellings adapted from metal grain silos. It was a heady era of social problem-solving, evidence of what a nation can do by focusing its talents, energies, and resources. Defense-industry towns were conceived and built as complete communities. The war acted as a catalyst for both

American corporations were forced to convert their peacetime assembly lines to war production, but they kept their names before the public through advertisements. In these ads, Nash-Kelvinator visually linked two sheet-metal icons of peace—the automobile and the refrigerator—with one of war—the bomber.

ICE CUBES FOR JAPAN !

Listen, Tojo—when you hear that *kur-rump* some night and the factory walls start sliding into the sea—look out, it's one of those new "ice cubes" from Nash-Kelvinator!

We are building *plenty* of them just for you—huge Kelvinators that fly and ice cubes that hurt.

Monster metal-bellied flying boats—growing on Nash-Kelvinator assembly lines—to whisk the Navy's men and material to any spot you raise your head! Giant Vought-Sikorsky cargo carriers built *complete*—and not in ones or twos, but in fleet upon fleet!

Want to hear some more?

Then listen—that angry hum coming out of the East—

They are the propellers built by Nash-Kelvinator, built by the many thousands!

And that mighty roar you'll soon be hearing is the voice of the most powerful engine ever placed in a pursuit ship. It will take the Navy's new *Corsair* higher, faster than any "Zero" in your stable.

They're coming, Tojo—coming from men who, in building last year's refrigerators and automobiles, thought only of a nation's health and happiness.

But now, it's hate and vengeance and the remembrance of a thousand Axis wrongs that are guiding their hands . . . beating every production record in Nash-Kelvinator history by two and three.

Look out, Tojo, *the nights are growing longer.*   • • •

NASH-KELVINATOR CORPORATION

NASH KELVINATOR

expansive postwar suburban development and modern architecture, incorporating the avant-garde into the mainstream. War-workers housing projects in Norfolk, Virginia, built early in the war by Levitt & Sons, anticipated in their mass-production construction techniques the vast postwar Levittowns. After the war, firms such as Skidmore, Owings & Merrill, architects of innumerable wartime projects, represented the best of a bureaucratic mode of architecture. They embraced the war's modernist aesthetics and functioned as big, corporate offices. On the other hand, architects like Louis I. Kahn, who had designed housing for war workers, reacted to the postwar hegemony of modernism by tempering it with historicist and monumental impulses.[2]

The war forged relationships between military, scientific, and academic interests. Corporate laboratories and individual inventors struggled to develop new materials and techniques such as Styrofoam, Saran, and molded plywood and to increase the productive capacity of existing materials such as fiberglass, aluminum, and acrylic sheeting. In those pre-environmentally conscious days, every new synthetic garnered praise and enthusiastic acceptance. "Is this *really* the age of plastics," Dow Chemical wondered in one of its many wartime ads. And thus it happened that when the war was over, progressive designers explored the aesthetic possibilities of these materials, creating now classic designs for modern living.

In pursuit of any technology that might have military applications, the United States created the Office of Scientific Research to coordinate a nationwide program. The fruits of this effort included the world's most advanced aircraft wind tunnel at the California Institute of Technology, laboratories for the development of radar, and three top-secret cities for the production and testing of atomic bombs. The bomb's strategic success made America the world's preeminent military power. Nuclear warfare convinced the country's leaders that scientific advances would play a major role in future confrontations, and this framework established a permanent cooperative of military, scientific and academic concerns. At the same time, and in a very profound way, the bomb changed forever our notion of the American land: with total annihilation from the air just a push-button away, we could never again speak with conviction of an isolated Fortress America.

WORLD WAR II AND THE AMERICAN DREAM

World War II radically dislocated the traditional roles of men and women, as the latter entered the work force in unprecedented numbers. Even women who stayed at home performed war work by growing victory gardens, recycling scrap metals, and conserving critical materials.

Modern, industrialized warfare had demanded a logistical infrastructure to ease the flow of men and materials. In 1942, a tri-level highway interchange, reportedly the nation's first, was built near the Willow Run bomber plant to accommodate the thousands of workers who commuted there. Such sprawling road systems constructed near some war plants became templates for the interstate highways that began to snake across the country in the 1950s.

But the war's turnaround was not achieved without social costs. "Ordinary citizens were lost," novelist James Jones later recalled, "in the almost incomprehensible boom and mass movement, trying to pick their way uphill through the crush to some island of security, in a new world that seemed to have gone crazy with both destruction and a lavish prosperity. This wrenching social upheaval and realignment, as much as the fact of the war itself, accounted for an almost total breakdown of the moral standard of prewar U.S. living. And nothing would ever quite be the same again."[3]

Massive wartime migration revealed a host of urban problems. Labor and housing shortages propelled formerly "unacceptable" workers like women and minorities into the labor force. At some West Coast shipyards, "Rosie the Riveter"'s comprised a quarter of the total work force by 1944, while the wartime influx of minorities into traditional all-white industries touched racial nerves. Chester Himes's novel, *If He Hollers Let Him Go* (1945), conflates these two situations when a white female worker at a Los Angeles shipyard falsely accuses a successful black foreman of rape and hence precipitates his personal disintegration. Real-life incidents reinforced Himes's fictional account. In 1943 there were race riots in Detroit, New York, and other major cities. The volatility of wartime employment and housing challenged notions of race and gender, presaging radical upheavals to come. After the end of World War II working women, forced to return home or to accept jobs that paid less than those they held during the war, anticipated their feminist daughters of the 1960s. And it is no coincidence that Ralph Ellison began his epochal novel of African-American consciousness, *Invisible Man*, in 1945.

However, publicity surrounding America's construction program was overwhelmingly patriotic, elevating the war into a symbol of the country's technological and organizational prowess. The greatly increased speed of modern warfare gave new resonance to the industrial design concept of planned obsolescence. Thus, as early as the fall of 1942, *Popular Mechanics* anticipated a postwar design culture of plug-in disposability, announcing that future home buyers would shop for residences "supplied by a mass-production corporation which turns out dwellings just as automobile companies rolled cars from the assembly line before the war."[4]

Such optimistic media, reinforced by turbulent wartime change, enshrined a notion of accelerated progress in the nation's collective psyche. Annihilate the old—wartime rhetoric encouraged—and you hasten the new. Wartime achievements thus led the public to expect a new age of plenty after years of sacrifice and hardship, and an ever-expanding abundance seemed the just reward following a war fought to protect the American way of life.

1. Attributed to Lindburgh's journal in Don Sherman, "Willow Run," *Air and Space* (August–September 1992): 79.
2. Henry-Russell Hitchcock proposed this postwar paradigm in "The Architecture of Bureaucracy and the Architecture of Genius," *Architectural Review* (January 1947): 3–6. I am indebted to Joan Ockman for bringing this to my attention.
3. *James Jones Reader*, ed. James R. Giles and J. Michael Lennon (New York: Carol Publishing Group, 1991), 267.
4. "Your Home of the Future," *Popular Mechanics* (October 1942): 72–77, 166.

Donald Albrecht is an architect and curator and a writer for Architecture *and other architectural journals. He is the curator of* World War II and the American Dream: How Wartime Building Changed a Nation, *an exhibition at the National Building Museum. This article is adapted from his introduction to the exhibition catalog, which is copublished by the National Building Museum and MIT Press. This essay is especially indebted to the research and insights of the exhibition's historian and catalog contributor, Joel Davidson, as well as to the contributions of catalog essayists Margaret Crawford, Robert Friedel, Greg Hise, Peter S. Reed, and Michael Sorkin. The exhibition and catalog were made possible by the Legacy Resource Management Program of the Department of Defense. Additional funding was provided by the Martin Marietta Corporation, the College of Fellows of the American Institute of Architects, and the United States Gypsum Company. The National Building Museum also wishes to acknowledge the assistance of the National Park Service.*

Bunkering the Poor:
Our Fortified Ghettos

Camilo José Vergara

At 2258 Mack Avenue on Detroit's east side there stands a 120-year-old gray wooden cottage, a former farmhouse. The roof has black holes left from a fire that raged on the afternoon of 17 February 1993. The glass windowpanes are gone, but the metal bars are still visible. "A sad day," says Ms. Jones, a neighbor. "All I could see was the smoke. The bars stopped them, the smoke killed them. It made me sick. I had to go to bed."

Outside, around the cottage, are mementos placed there by people trying to come to terms with the tragedy: a red ribbon tied to the doorknob; stuffed animals arranged on the front steps; a bright yellow tricycle parked in the weeds; a table with a large clock, its hands stuck at two o'clock, the time of the fire; and next to it a neat line of children's shoes. A crude billboard depicts the faces of three angelic children; four ovals, each framing a cross, represent the others.

LaWanda Williams, age 9; Nikia Williams, 7; Dakwan Williams, 6; La Quinten Lyons, 4; Venus Lyons, 2; Anthony Lyons, 7 months; and Mark Brayboy, 2 died when left alone in their "prison house." In the preceding five months another six people in Detroit, most of them children, had also died trapped by fires in barred and barricaded houses.

Fortification epitomizes the ghetto in America today, just as back alleys, crowded tenements, and lack of play areas defined

Defended mailboxes, South Bronx. In this drug-infested building, mail is delivered to a separate locked room.

the slum of the late nineteenth century. Buildings grow claws and spikes, their entrances acquire metal plates, their roofs get fenced in, and any additional openings are sealed, cutting down on light and ventilation. Glass windowpanes in first-floor windows are rare. Instead, window openings are bricked in or fitted with glass bricks. In schools and in buses, Plexiglas, frosty with scratches, blurs the view outside.

Even in areas where statistics show a decrease in major crime, fortification continues to escalate, and as it does ghettos lose their coherence. Neighborhoods are replaced by a random assortment of isolated bunkers, structures that increasingly resemble jails or power stations, their interiors effectively separated from the outside. Throughout the nation's cities we are witnessing the physical hardening of a new order—streetscapes so menacing, so alien, that they would not be tolerated if they were found anywhere besides poor, minority communities. In brick and cinder block and sharpened metal, inequality takes material form.

The United States Post Office is the main symbol of the federal government in the ghetto. But where one might expect reassuring classical buildings decorated with eagles and images of the old Pony Express, there are instead squat concrete block buildings with iron grating. The only unifying national symbols are the American flag on the outside and, on the inside, the FBI most-wanted poster.

In a truly democratic society there would be no great differences in the quality of government buildings. The post office constructs for the same purpose in different communities. Yet in the ghetto, form does not follow function so much as it does fear. A building's adaptations for survival announce the existence of a state of urban war, a fact that even Washington cannot ignore.

"Post offices should look friendly, identifiable, efficient, and stylistically typical of local buildings—not like factories," concluded a study published in 1989 in *Progressive Architecture*. Certainly, the fortresslike ghetto post office is "stylistically typical." The same can be said of the most modest representation of the postal system: apartment building mailboxes, which are often covered by a locked iron grid. In dangerous buildings in New York City, the boxes are kept in a separate locked room.

Commercial establishments in U.S. ghettos are just as heavily defended. In 1975, businessman Phillip Cyprian of Gary, Indiana figured that even if his clothing store were housed in an all steel building with no windows or doors, burglars would still find a way to enter and clean him out. "They'd take cutting torches and do it and never get caught," he reasoned. So Cyprian decided to move out of Gary. Entrepreneurs who stayed behind have applied measures only a little less drastic than those in Cyprian's bleak architectural vision. "We try to block anything at all that can give people the idea this place is an easy target," explains the owner of a warehouse in Camden, New Jersey. In Detroit, a fenced roof, blocked windows, and a jail door help to make Singleton Cleaners a difficult target, while its bright colors announce to drivers that the establishment is indeed in business. At a Newark Kentucky Fried Chicken franchise, a large plastic menu is protected with Plexiglas and an iron grating, obscuring much of the writing. Interiors have also been modified. In businesses and public offices, bullet-proof Plexiglas separates attendants and clients; people are buzzed in only after being screened by a receptionist.

Churches also turn into fortresses. In Brownsville, Brooklyn, St. Luke's Community Church, formerly a Jewish catering hall, had the misfortune of being located across the street from a rubble-filled vacant lot. After school, neighborhood children threw bricks at the church, breaking windows; so the congregation simply blocked them. The Lighthouse Gospel M.B. Church in Chicago gets a little daylight through a cross made of glass bricks.

Most of these structures are accented by razor-ribbon wire. It was not until the late 1970s that this wire, formerly common only in prisons and military installations, came into large-scale use for civilian purposes. First strung atop fences around warehouses and factories, it has more recently become a favorite device for domestic defense, separating roofs of adjacent apartment buildings, securing the space between structures, and protecting their perimeters. Yet despite awesome fortifications, buildings are still broken into and burned, and the streets, now invisible to those inside, are even more threatening.

Greater Holy Light Missionary Baptist Church, South-Central Los Angeles

U.S. Post Office, designed for the dangers of the ghetto, South Bronx. A local resident commented, "It seems that they are afraid of thieves."

BUNKERING THE POOR

Highbridge Branch of the New York Public Library, South Bronx

With a capacity for over 200 families, this HELP College Avenue family shelter is the largest, most expensive, and most formidable of the new facilities in the South Bronx.

CAMILO JOSÉ VERGARA   23

Some choice public spaces are open for only a few hours during the day, while others are allowed to fall into disrepair, to harbor drug dealers, and to function as open dumps. In "people's parks"—places accessible only with a key—those enjoying the green grass, trees, and flowers seem to be themselves part of an exhibit for passers-by. Fences dwarf the tiny spaces.

Within such environments, police are perceived as distant, taking a long time to answer calls and often refusing to come at night. Dogs and security guards protect the few who can afford them. And, if one is to believe residents, just about everybody keeps a gun. Thus people defend their homes. Those living in town houses and private dwellings surround the borders of their property with fences enclosing the house and family car. In addition, they bar their first-floor windows and often install clearly visible burglar alarms, red lights blinking.

In South-Central Los Angeles a basic fortress is a bungalow with a small green lawn. The dwelling's first line of defense is an iron door, usually painted black. Metal bars on the windows add further protection, changing the once-friendly character of the wood and stucco houses. Less visible are the iron spikes to ward off trespassers.

In urban sections where apartment buildings are the characteristic abode, outsiders are discouraged from entering by locked extensions made of iron fencing that juts out, removing sections of sidewalk from public use. Where there were courtyard entrances, there are now heavy gates topped with razor-ribbon wire. Inside buildings, a guard dog chained to the stairway railing calls attention to suspicious movements. In dangerous housing projects, metal doors to apartments have as many as four locks, including one at the center that releases two cross-shaped bars. Between the dogs and the door locks, however, are often-dark hallways, and little can be done to defend those.

Despite the profusion of physical barriers against crime, the most effective defense is social, as people watch after one another's dwellings, question strangers, and call the police. In violent neighborhoods in New York City, Newark, and Chicago, social arrangements have evolved that befit a state of war. Groups of disabled and elderly residents going from their secure buildings to check-cashing outlets and the supermarket require police or security guards for escorts. At the entrance of shelters and welfare offices, guards face photographs and composite drawings of people wanted for crimes.

Milagros Jimenez—a small, middle-aged woman, the president of her building's tenant association, and a South Bronx resident—tells of her courageous struggle to save her building. "I would go with Gladys to the roof at two or three in the morning to watch so that people would not go there to do drugs and kick out those who were doing drugs. Since we were with God and I was with another brave person, I was not afraid."

People also resort to religion and magic. As protection against evil, Elizabeth Valentin, also a resident of the South Bronx, keeps saints and voodoo statues by her bed. She credits these images with having saved her during at least five muggings.

Signs are widely used as warnings. A piece of cardboard on an apartment window of a Chicago Housing Authority project, Altgeld Gardens in South Riverdale, reads, "No Trespassing. Due to an epidemic of AIDS do not enter my apartment when I am absent. Game is over, dude." Other prominently displayed notices alert intruders that they will be attacked by dogs or even shot. A warning sign in front of a house on Hillman Avenue in Youngstown, Ohio, reads,

Yo' Homes, rock starz, body sellarz, bad boyz
Do NOT
1. "CHILL" Here
2. "CLOCK" Here
3. "HANG TUFF"
4. SELL rockz HERE
5. READ too LONG
In other words
STROLL!
Yes, this means you 2

Yet even these kinds of signs, as well as letters and numbers bearing the names, addresses, and purposes of edifices, are often stripped by thieves and vandals.

Concern for security has led to a new brutalism. Fortification creates a conflict between the desire to make people feel welcome and the grim need for defense. Those who live or work in such buildings say that outside appearance has little to do with the quality of what is offered inside. The manager of a forbidding day shelter in Chicago declares himself proud of offering the best meals of any shelter in the city. A recreation worker at the Hillside Community Center, which looms like an arsenal on Milwaukee's north side, boasts that great basketball games are played inside. And a South Bronx resident comments that despite the menacing claws on the roof and metal shutters on the windows, her neighborhood public library is always busy.

Those involved in the erection of fortresses deny that their buildings are in any way extraordinary. A Salvation Army official who took part in designing a bunkerlike building in Chicago explained, "There are windows there—a clerestory window in the chapel above, and small windows along the side. We don't spend enormous amounts on large windows, but to call this building a fortress seems to be a little overkill. It is not like a Strategic Air Command blockhouse, where I served when I was in the service, where you work in the basement and you have to go upstairs to see if the sun ever came up that day."

A South Bronx resident was so surprised by what she heard about the High Bridge Branch of the New York Public Library that she "had to come here and check it out and take some books out." Another, commenting on the metal spikes that ring the roof's perimeter, said, "It is sad, isn't it? I guess they don't want people on the roof." A guard at the Office of Family Services in the South Bronx laughed at the comparison between his workplace and a prison, saying, "Too small for a jail—it does not cover enough ground. In New York you never find a jail this small." Yet most people interviewed perceived that the defenses were there to protect them, and nobody expressed a wish that they be removed. Instead, people strive to soften the unfriendliness of their environments, decorating homes and businesses with lively paintings, ornate wrought iron designs, and plantings. But outside of this, the fortress remains.

Plans that a quarter century ago gave rise to polemics against the "school of brutalism" that was so prominent in the 1960s have become widely accepted in ghetto neighborhoods. "It is strange that those designs that were made to provoke an outrageous response should become everyday normality—what you have to have to get through the day," remarked Marshall Berman, professor of political science at City College in New York.

What does it mean to live in a windowless world lined with sharp things that protect by threatening to cut, puncture, and impale? A world characterized by animals that bark and bite, crude warning signs, bars that keep some out but may also prevent escape? A world defined by security guards and razor-ribbon wire, by streets, hallways, and nights that don't belong to you? People in these neighborhoods express their dislike of fortification but accept it as inevitable.

Fortification has profound consequences. Where defenses are aggressively displayed they create bizarre, shunned streetscapes of distorted survivors and ruined losers. The time spent opening and closing so many locks and gates, connecting and disconnecting alarms, nervously looking over one's shoulder, feeding guard dogs, and explaining one's business to security personnel can become exhausting and detract from other activities. Blocking the openings in buildings forces people to consume more electricity for artificial lighting and cooling, while increasing their isolation and sense of imprisonment. Scarce resources that should be devoted to basic needs and services are used instead for security and fortification. And residents feel powerless in their cages because they believe that crime is out of control.

Detroit's 2258 Mack Avenue has an aura. Terrible images pass through one's mind upon seeing the broken, old-fashioned cottage surrounded by tokens of sorrow. A few blocks east, on the corner of Meldrum, the writing on the wall of an abandoned building says, "We remember that when people lose their lives as a consequence of injustice their spirit wanders, unable to pass ever-seeking resolution." The message is repeated clearly and neatly several times to make sure someone notices.

This text is an edited version of "Our Fortified Ghettos," originally published in The Nation 258 (31 January 1994): 121–24.

Camilo José Vergara is a writer and photojournalist who has been documenting poor minority communities for seventeen years. His latest book, The New American Ghetto, *will be published in 1995 by Rutgers University Press.*

Beyond Dystopia, Beyond Theory Formation

Richard Plunz

Mott Haven in the South Bronx is a place that defies even the notion of dystopia; it indicates that ghettos and the so-called "theory formation" of recent note in architectural and cultural studies do not necessarily mix. The images that follow are from a 1991 study of Mott Haven. We recorded the epochal situation of United States urbanism without adornment, theoretical or otherwise. In what other city in the history of the world can one construct such images? Actually, in Detroit, or Los Angeles, . . .

This analytic work was performed between September and November 1991 by Columbia University architecture students with Richard Plunz as critic and with the collaboration of Camilo José Vergara, photographer, and Leonard Hicks, UNIDOS Community Organization, Mott Haven. The work was created on GSDL 3D modeling software provided by GIST, Inc., and generated on Silicon Graphics IRIS work stations at the Columbia University GSAPP computer facility under the direction of Christos Tountas with Eden Muir. It was shown with the New American Ghetto exhibition, which was also designed by the Columbia University students, at the StoreFront for Art and Architecture (November–January 1991).

Richard Plunz is an architect and professor of architecture and director of the Urban Design Program at the Graduate School of Architecture at Columbia University. He is the author of numerous studies on the correlation between physical and social design, including the 1992 A History of Housing in New York City (Columbia University Press).

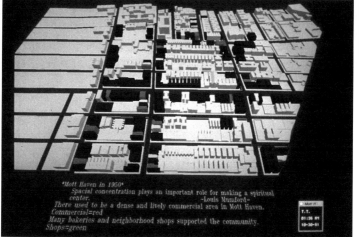

Mott Haven in 1950. "Spatial concentration plays an important role for making a spiritual center."—Louis Mumford. There used to be a dense and lively commercial area in Mott Haven. Commercial=black. Many bakeries and neighborhood shops supported the community. Shops=gray.

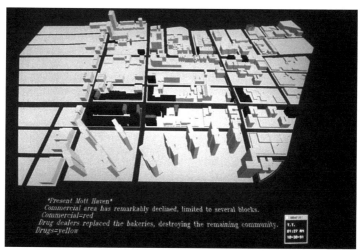

Present Mott Haven [1991]. Commercial area has remarkably declined, limited to several blocks. Commercial=black. Drug dealers replaced the bakeries, destroying the remaining community. Drugs=gray.

BEYOND DYSTOPIA, BEYOND THEORY FORMATION

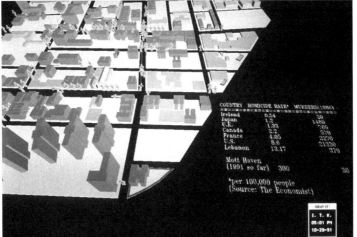

Murder rate per 100,000 people, 1986, source—The Economist

Country	Rate	Murders						
			U.K.	1.33	760	U.S.	8.60	21330
Ireland	0.54	20	Canada	2.20	570	Lebanon	13.17	370
Japan	1.20	1480	France	4.05	2270			

Murder rate per 100,000, January–November 1991   Mott Haven   300.00   36

Fires
Gray=one fire in 1991
Black=two or more fires in 1991
Outline=demolished due to fire during the last 20 years

Since January 1, 1991, 149 people have been shot in Mott Haven, 36 fatally. This is a homicide rate of over 300 per 100,000 people: over 20 times the rate of Lebanon, over 600 times the rate of Ireland.

149 shootings, 36 killings, 158 days—broken TV's, cardboard, crack vials, dead animals. Upon the devastation, the abandoned lots became huge dumping grounds for industrial, drug, and residential refuse. Aside from the haunting effect it creates in the neighborhood... aside from the bitterness it evokes in the community... aside from the demoralizing quality it imposes on the young... the refuse causes the street life in these areas to shift to the remaining congested areas where the shootings, the killings, and the robberies happen.

BEYOND DYSTOPIA, BEYOND THEORY FORMATION

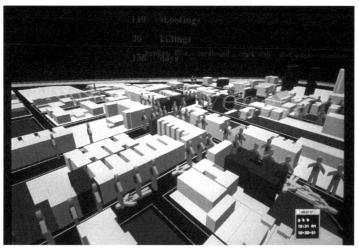

Gonzalo Benavides

149 shootings, 36 killings, 158 days—broken TV's, cardboard, crack vials, dead animals.

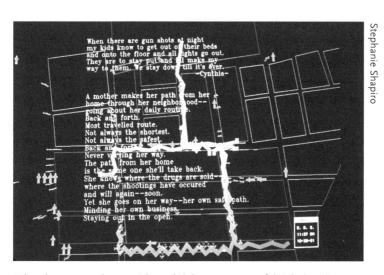

Stephanie Shapiro

When there are gun shots at night my kids know to get out of their beds and onto the floor and all lights go out. They are to stay put and I'll make my way to them. We stay down 'til it's over.—Cynthia
A mother makes her path from her home through her neighborhood—going about her daily routine. Back and forth. Most traveled route. Not always the shortest. Not always the safest. Back and forth. Never varying her way. The path from her home is the same one she'll take back. She knows where the drugs are sold—where the shootings have occurred and will again—soon. Yet she goes on her way—her own safe path. Minding her own business. Staying out in the open.

RICHARD PLUNZ

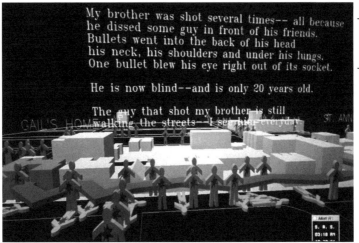

My brother was shot several times—all because he dissed some guy in front of his friends. Bullets went into the back of his head, his neck, his shoulders, and under his lungs. One bullet blew his eye right out of its socket. He is now blind—and is only 20 years old. The guy that shot my brother is still walking the streets—I see him every day.

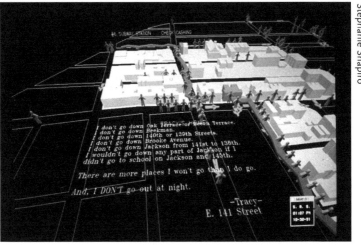

I don't go down Oak Terrace or Beech Terrace. I don't go down Beekman. I don't go down 140th or 139th streets. I don't go down Brooke Avenue. I don't go down Jackson from 141st to 138th. I wouldn't go down any part of Jackson if I didn't go to school on Jackson and 145th. There are more places I won't go than I do go. And, I DON'T go out at night.—Tracy, E. 141 Street

BEYOND DYSTOPIA, BEYOND THEORY FORMATION

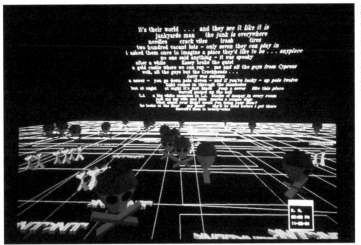

it's their world... and they see it like it is
junkyards man, the junk is everywhere
needles, crack viles, trash, tires
two hundred vacant lots—only seven they can play in
asked them once to imagine a place they'd like to be... anyplace
no one said anything—it was spooky
after a while, Kasey broke the quiet
a gold castle where we can rap—me and all the guys from Cypress
well, all the guys but the Crackheads...
Jerry was solemn
a sewer—you go down pole eleven—and if you're lucky—up pole twelve
light comes in through the manholes
but at night, at night it's just black, yeah a sewer, like this place
Darrell picked up the ball
L.A., a big white mansion in L.A., stacks of money in every room
just me my wife and kids, maybe a couple dogs
what about your mom? would you bring your mom?
he looks at the floor, my mom? she'll be dead before i get there
Darrell's mom is twenty-nine

RICHARD PLUNZ   35

Sarajevo Under Siege
Warchitecture

Tzar Mosque, built in 1565 • Gazi Husref-bey Library, built in 1565 • Gazi Husref-bey Mosque, built in 1530 • Gazi Husref-bey Turbe • Sheih Magribi Mosque, built in the fifteenth century • Ali-Pasha Mosque, built in 1561 • Havadza Durak Mosque (the mosque at the Bascarsija Market), built in the sixteenth century • Hanika'h (a Sufi school), dating from the sixteenth century • Gazi Husref-bey Medresa (school), built in 1537 • Islamic Faculty • Cekrekcija Mosque, built in 1526 • Ferhad-bey Mosque (Ferhadija), built in 1561–62 • Hadzi-Osman Mesjid (Tabacki), built in 1591–92 • Coban-Hassan-Vojvoda Mosque (Cobanija), built in 1562 • Dzindo-Zade Mosque (Dzanic Mosque) and Asikovac, built in the seventeenth century • Dajanli Hadzi-Ibrahim Mosque at Gorica, dating from the seventeenth century • Hadzi-Sinan Teki, dating from the seventeenth century • Divan-Katib Hajdar Mosque ("White Mosque") at Vratnik • Kovaci Mosque • Gazgani Hadzi-Ali Mesjid at Sirokaca, dating from 1561 • Hrasno Mosque • Sheriat Law School, built in 1887 • Sarac Ali Mosque at Vrbanjusa, built in 1892–93 • new Kobilja Glava Mosque • Svraka Village Mosque • Ugorsko Village Mosque • Semizovac Mosque • Sokolje Village Mosque • New Buljakov Potok Mosque • Brijesce Mosque • Butmir Mosque • New Kotorac Mosque • Sheij Faruh Mosque (Abdesthana) at Kovaci, built in 1541 • Hadzi Inhan-aga Topalovic Mosque (Lubo Mosque) at Vratnik,

Commercial and residential building, Racher-babic

built in 1525 • Sinan Vojvoda Hatun Mosque ("Under-the-Walnut Mosque" or "Little Mosque") at Vratnik-Mejdan, built in 1552 • Hadzi Sinan Mokrica Mesjid in Vratnik • Kasaf-Zade Mosque at Vratnik • Hadzi-Ibrahim Kasapovic Mesjid at Vratnik, built in the sixteenth century • Gazi Husref-bey Endowment Administration Building (Vakuf) • Morica han, built in the sixteenth century • City Market Building, built in 1895 • Customs and Financial Services Headquarters, built in 1891 • Esad efedi Kulovic Building, built in 1897 • Prison-Beledija Town Hall, built in 1895 • Society Club and Theater, built in 1897 • Grand Hotel, built in 1893–95 • El. Generating Plant Administrative Building, built in 1894 • Hotel National • Evangelistic Church, built in 1899 • School of Sheriat-Islamic laws, built in 1887 • Elementary school for Boys, built in 1893 • Villa of the Bosnian-Herzegovinian Clerk Retirement Endowment • Petra Pesut Residential and Office Building, built in 1898–1900 • Palace of Territorial Government, built in 1884–85 • Cathedral, built in 1884–89 • Gazi-Ishak Bet Spa, built in 1890 • Ajac-Pasha Court, Hotel Central, built in 1889 • Dr. Berthold Kraso House, built in 1897 • Daniel Moris Salom Residential and Office Building, built in 1897 • Archbishop Seminary and St. Cyril and Method Church, built in 1892–96 • Town Hall, built in 1891–96 • Bascarsija public drinking fountain, built in 1891 • Pension Fund Building, built in 1891 • Mithropolis Palace, built in 1898 • Hotel Europe, built in 1881–82 • Costa Hörmann Villa, built in 1890 • Joseph and Julia Never Residential and Office Building, built in 1894 • Giuseppe and Vitta Salom House, built in 1881 • Petar Todorovic Residential and Office Building, built in 1894 • Omer Kramarovic Office Building, built in 1897 • Mihail Pregrada House and Carpenter Workshop, built in 1892 • Grigorije Hadziseferdzi Residential and Office Building, built in 1890 • August and Maria Braun Residential and Office Building, built in 1895 • Territorial Hospital, built in 1892–94 • Franichevich Residential Building, built in 1912 • Halid Dvor, built in 1913 • Rasema Svro-Comara Building, built in 1898 • Jeshua D. Salom Palace, built in 1901 • Hinko Shlesinger House and Pharmacy, built in 1902 • Isaac A. Salom Building, built in 1903 • Moris A. Kabiljo Building, built in 1903 • Hieronim G. Salom Building, built in 1903 • Ante Stambuk Building, built in 1905 • steam mill, built in 1909 • Main Post Office (formerly Military and Telegraph Office), built in 1907–13 • School for Nuns, built in 1904 • Holy Trinity Church, built in 1904–06 • Church of St. Rosary, built in 1911 • St. Ante Padovanski Church, built in 1911 • Hermina Radisch House, built in 1903 • Anton Luzina House, built in 1904 • Artur Popper House, built in 1903 • Joseph Sabataj Finci Building, built in 1906 • Dr. Jozo Sunaric Villa, built in 1911 • Isidor Israel Building, built in 1910 • Central Bank of Croatia Building, built in 1912 • Subsidiary of the Austro-Hungarian Bank Building, built in 1912 • Jovo Samoukovic Building, built in 1901 • Sinan M. Besarovic Building • Danes-Lah Building, built in 1906 • Jeshua and Mojca Salom House, built in 1912 • Isak Salom House, built in 1911 • Abdaga Sahinagic House, built in 1908 • Dr. Fisher School and Club, built in 1909 • Vailikije Petrovic House, built in 1907 • Salom Palace, built in 1911 • Hadin Ali-Pash Vakuf Building, built in 1910. These historic buildings in Sarajevo were destroyed, set on fire, or considerably damaged.

The following images are from Warchitecture-Sarajevo: A Wounded City, *a multimedia exhibition documenting the destruction of architecture in Sarajevo through photographs, publication, films, audiotape, and personal testimony. Created by the Bosnia-Herzegovina Association of Architects (Das-Sabih) in Sarajevo between May 1992 and October 1993,* Warchitecture *describes the combined physical and psychological assault against the civilian population by presenting one of the main forms of aggression: the destruction of the city's architecture. On 16 March 1994, five members of Das-Sabih—Midhat Cesovic, Borislav Curic, Nasif Hasanbegovic, Darko Serfic, and Sabahundin Spilja—escaped with the exhibition packed in two crates. To inform the general public and professionals about the degeneration of Sarajevo and to establish contacts that hopefully would lead to the reconstruction of the city, they presented the exhibition at the arc en reve centre d'architecture in Bordeaux, France; at the Centre Georges Pompidou in Paris; and subsequently at numerous other museums and galleries in Europe.* Warchitecture *was presented at StroreFront for Art and Architecture from 4 February–18 March 1995.*

National and University Library

SARAJEVO UNDER SIEGE

Assembly and Government Building of the Republic of Bosnia-Herzegovina

Unioninvest Headquarters

Sarajevo City Museum

SARAJEVO UNDER SIEGE

Ali-Pasha Mosque

Main Post Office (formerly Military and Telegraph Office)

Gazi Husref-bey Mosque

SARAJEVO UNDER SIEGE

Olympic Sports Hall ("Zetra")

Sports and Cultural Center ("Syenderija") Youth Club

Everyday War

Lebbeus Woods

The statement "Architecture is war. War is architecture."[1] has upset many people. War, it seems, occupies a particular place in human experience that peace does not. It is an echo of the awesome, the terrible, and the sublime that Edmund Burke, among others, reserved for special occasions. An equation of war and peace seems to offend this idea of war. Even more, it challenges the idea of the normal, for it seems that this category, which embraces, none too lovingly, the everyday and the ordinary, is something to be held outside of the sublime. Yet the offending statement proposes exactly the opposite—that war and peace are intertwined in direct and interdependent ways. It is as much to say that peace involves war, and the converse, that war contains a particular kind of peace.

Those who recall slogans of the Orwellian dystopia will detect a measure of "doublethink" in this corollary remark. And doublethink it is. Poor George simply was unable to enjoy the fact. He believed it was dictatorship that would most benefit from the exploitation of paradoxical thinking, simply because dictators choose to lie so much. The only "opposite" he could imagine was "truth"—objective truth, that is, which has never been more than the truth of those holding power at the moment. But lies are in no way paradoxical. Lies do not, as he exposed so clearly, express the condition of "holding two contradictory concepts in the mind at the same time, and believing both." Lies, or at least those made by the dictators he had in mind, are never believed by the liars. Rather, they are used to obscure an actuality. In this way, every lie confirms a truth. The liar is perhaps the greatest believer in truth, simply because he struggles so hard to conceal it. Rather, in doublethink, Orwell unintentionally introduced a more complex and subtle concept than mere lying. To hold two contradictory concepts in the mind at the same time, and to believe in both—that is closer to poesis than to crude propaganda. Indeed, it is the very essence of living.

In fact this concept best serves those individuals and societies (though there are none purely of this kind today) that are devoted to the liberation of the human mind. Living things, contrary to Aristotle's logical constrictions, not only are filled with contradictions, but thrive on them. The second law of his logic (and let no one today believe that this law is no longer absolutely in force) dictates that a cannot equal b, because a equals a; that is, persons and things have fixed "identities." But however expedient this belief may be in solving logical problems, it overlooks the fact that every person and thing is constantly changing, becoming "something else." For example, does not a person's body, which is considered integral with personhood when alive, become a mere thing when the person dies?

The attempt to salvage identity and the logic underlying it leads, in this case, to Descartes's duality, which is as arid and damaging a concept to the idea of liberation as has ever existed. A simpler example: a person is walking across the room. At any instance, is he "only" at a particular place in the room, one defined, say, by Cartesian coordinates? If so, how does he get to the next place—in other words, how does he cross the threshold of the limits of the increment? And where is he when he does? Between coordinates? Well, where, in such a system of logical description, is that? "Becoming"—whether in the form of simple motion or historical transformation—cannot be divided into discrete increments of identity, but flows as a continuum, so that at any one "point" (the concept of which is no more than a logical convenience) a thing is simultaneously what it "is" and what it is "becoming." Identities are transformational, sliding and shifting in an ongoing complex stream of becoming. In the continuum of living, a, it seems does equal b.

But perhaps this is where Orwell has a point—a does not actually "equal" b; nor does war "equal" peace anymore than ignorance "is" power. An equation inevitably opposes two entities, and this opposition, made to prove equivalency, invariably proves non-equivalency just as well. For no matter how thoroughly it is proven that two entities are equivalent, the question of their fixity at any "point" in the (re)solution returns the problem to its Aristotelian, noncontradictory form. Yet it is precisely a form of fixed identity that is lost (or perhaps it is better to say never gained) in the onrush of time and events. Things are not equivalent to one another, therefore maintaining separate and isolated existences; rather they are *part* of one another. Furthermore, they cannot be divided, except at the convenience of a particular verbal or mathematical language. It is in the context of this argument that war and architecture should be considered.

In particular, the ideas commonly described as "construction" and "destruction" need to be examined in the context of the paradoxicality inherent in experience. Few thoughtful people would fail to acknowledge that in order to build, something must be destroyed. Architects speak of ecological concerns today in a rather thoughtless way, believing that their buildings are energy efficient, use "natural" materials, do not pollute the environment, and so on. They are speaking in relative terms, of course, not only because the act of building and its consequences still create waste and pollution and remain highly "unnatural," but also because they introduce new forms of entropy into the existing environment. Not only do "natural" materials involve the mining of the earth and the felling of forests, resulting in the disruption of plant and animal life, the pollution of rivers and air, and the degradation of human existence, which is dependent upon these natural resources, but they produce buildings that begin to decay even as they are built. The effects of this decay, which continues regardless of all efforts at maintenance, contribute to the spiral of human life, indeed of the whole environment, downward towards an ultimate heat death. Far-fetched as this may sound, it need not be understood only in millennial terms. Anyone who has studied the nature of buildings understands their relatively short life spans. These are measured not only in terms of the wearing-out or erosion of materials, but in their lack of durability in terms of use. The average life span of a building built in any city today is twenty-five years. After that, it will most likely be torn down, if not simply abandoned. In the former case, an entire industry has been created to deal with the dross of used-up buildings; in the latter, an industry of bureaucratic sloth. It is not too much, in light of these facts, to say that buildings are built in order to be destroyed, or at least partly so. Destruction is factored in, at the very least, to construction. They are inevitably and paradoxically intertwined.

But this is not the only paradox to be realized. Building is by its very nature an aggressive, even warlike act. For one thing, buildings are objects that disrupt existing landscapes. Older buildings, perhaps much-loved, must be torn down. Fields and farms are taken over. But perhaps, it can be argued, the reasons for building are benevolent ones. A certain type of building is "needed." But who needs this building? And who will *not* get a building they need in order that those who can command a building into existence get theirs? No society is rich enough to build all the buildings it "needs," if, that is, it takes into account the demands of all its people. A building will only be beautiful and useful for those who benefit directly and tangibly from its existence. As for others, blind to its benefits because they occur at the expense of those that might have been their own, the building is little more than an instrument of denial. But at great expense and on a monumental scale, it is also nothing less than an instrument of war.

This is no mere metaphor. Marshall Berman describes the war conducted by Robert Moses and the authority he controlled on many New York neighborhoods in the 1940s and 1950s.[2] The wrecking machines that leveled houses and urban blocks were no less destructive to culture than if they had been the tanks and artillery of an attacking army. The finished highways and parks, purportedly benefits for the masses, were actually monuments to the victory of autocratic authority over the fragile lives of mere people. Even granting that every act of construction is not as wantonly indifferent to an existing fabric of culture as this, the fact that every building aggressively destroys such a fabric, even if only a little, cannot be denied. Nor can it be denied that the fabric destroyed is always that of an "inferior" class of culture (whether it be agrarian or simply old and in the way of progress), or of people (whether they be the wrong color or economic circumstances). The building of architecture is essentially political and, even though it is rarely presented as such, ideological. It is by nature warlike in the violence of its clearing of a site, the sheer energy of its construction, and the naked exercise of its power to change social and environmental conditions.

But there is a more profound paradox lying in wait between war and architecture. This is to be found in the destruction of an idea of normal that their correspondence brings. In short, the everyday is not innocent of the violence by which war is usually stigmatized, or elevated, depending on point of view; it merely conceals domestic violence and other forms of physical and emotional aggression under the label "abnormal." The "normal" actually consists of routines, procedures, protocols, manners, and customs that create the appearance of some fundamental relationships between the people of a culture and are asserted as being "true"[3] by their universal nature. In fact, this commonality has nothing to do with the actual relationships between people, or the lack of them. Indeed, people hardly know, or even see, each other. What they have in common, besides the conventions that they are more or less coerced into observing, is exactly their lack of commonality—which is to say, their uniqueness and individuality. By disrupting or destroying the comforting, repetitious patterns of conventional thought and behavior, war in effect strips away the mask of the normal, revealing an actuality that is both liberating and terrifying.

To survive in war means to become extremely conscious of one's particular place and movements, of one's every decision, need, and action—in other words, to become much more independent and self-aware, and, in very tangible terms, self-responsible. This is liberating because consciousness is heightened; emotions and reasonings are necessarily more sharp, precise, and consequential. In taking personal responsibility for one's own survival, one feels in certain ways stronger and more in control. At the same time, the loss of a set pattern of predictability, of the sense that one is acting within a larger social whole in which responsibilities are shared, can be terrifying. The feeling of being alone, vulnerable, and isolated within the limitations of one's own individuality and abilities cannot help but produce anxiety and alienation. The loss of the normal is a loss of innocence that can never be recovered.

As a result of war, architecture, too, suffers this loss. Formerly it could be concerned simply with enhancing the normal, with giving routine behavior and cultural conventions aesthetic qualities that seem to elevate them beyond the power of their own monotonous claim to innocence. By exalting the everyday activities of people and the social institutions that direct them, architecture could dignify them, reinforcing their truth. It could suggest that life, even at its most ordinary, was worth living because it is part of a much larger world whose beauty, taken as a whole, is inaccessible, yet can still be glimpsed in moments of "good design."4 During war, "good design" can only refer to lost innocence. In the aftermath of war, it can only be reinstituted with a substantial degree of disingenuousness. What is called for then is neither something "good" nor "true," but rather something paradoxically human: an architecture of liberation and terror.5

Alas, the poor architects—how roughly war treats them! It not only takes the moral high ground from under them, but it demands that they, like all those who are forced to come face to face with the harsher conditions of existence, painstakingly revise the superstructures of their practices and precepts—in short, their very conception of architecture, and of themselves. Everyday war is the worst. Where once they could believe they were creating beauty, raising humanity to a higher standard of living or even a higher level of existence—all of which might, on occasion, be true—they (or at least those with eyes to see) must become aware that in so doing they are soldiers in an army engaged in the conquest of space, and at the command of very particular individuals and institutions, whose ends, if they are to be realized, must be pursued ruthlessly, in other words, in the name of many. Whose idea of "beauty" is being served? Who benefits when the dust has settled? Whose idea of "higher" was monumentalized through immense expenditure of human lives and resources? What was lost in order that some could gain?

EVERYDAY WAR

The answers to these questions are not as clear as the individuals and institutions, the clients of architecture, would have the architects believe. Far from it, they can only be reached through an endless maze of questions and personal choices.

All of this is not to say that construction equals destruction, but only that they are, paradoxically, part of one another. "Architecture is war. War is architecture."—the first phrase would make no sense without the one that follows it. This does not imply that architects should not build, or that they should not lend themselves to wars between cultures, classes, and ideas, but only that they should not deceive themselves about what they are doing, and why. They should make their choices consciously, honestly, and with their eyes open, accepting personal responsibility for what they do. Today, this is seldom the case. If it were, the likelihood is that more well-intentioned architects would not choose to build what they do.

1. Lebbeus Woods, *War and Architecture/Rat I Arhitektura*, Pamphlet Architecture 15 (New York: Princeton Architectural Press, 1993), 1.
2. Marshall Berman, *All That Is Solid Melts Into Air: The Experience of Modernity* (New York: Penguin Books, 1988), 290–312.
3. Freud made a thorough study of "obsessive-compulsive" behavior, which, like routinized, conventionalized behavior, is rooted in the desire to remain innocent. In the former case, one wants to remain innocent of one's anger; in the latter case, of one's anxiety. In both cases, these "negative" emotions are feared as being overwhelming.
4. The use of the word "good" is revealing in this context, for it carries with it a moral connotation, as opposed to "excellent" or "useful," which are more descriptive. But if one is an "excellent" person or "useful," this does not necessarily imply that they are "good." "Good design" is design that confirms the "truth," that is, the body of conventions held in common.
5. As the author has argued in *War and Architecture*.

Lebbeus Woods is an architect, writer, and professor of architecture at The Cooper Union.

Balkanization and the Postmodern City

D. G. Shane

Preface

The late Robin Evans, shortly before his death in February 1993, gave a lecture at The Architectural League of New York in which he argued that we live in an age of pacification, despite all the evidence to the contrary (see Kathy Chia, "In Case You Missed It . . . " *Oculus* vol. 55, no. 6 [February 1993]: 4). Listening to my old friend was difficult: how could he think of cubist fragmentation, collage city, and deconstruction as similar aesthetic masks for a larger process of pacification? It was hard to see his logic in the face of a wave of homicides, violence, and riots in the United States and a campaign of ethnic cleansing that was destroying a 500-year-old, multicultural, hybrid heritage in the former Yugoslavia. What follows is in part a tribute to my friend and a meditation upon his provocative statement.

Evans could speak with authority about pacification. His pioneering archival research on Jeremy Bentham's Penitentiary Panopticon twenty-five years ago (later published as *The Fabrication of Virtue: English Prison Architecture 1750–1840* [Cambridge University Press, 1982]) had provided Michel Foucault with the prime carceral model of totalitarian control and centralized, dominant, optical inspection in the Enlightenment. The radial plan of this prison allowed inmates to be controlled in their cells by the gaze of a single, hidden, central jailer. Evans emphasized

French Hospital of Sarajevo

the importance of this scopic regime in Bentham's social engineering theories as well as the isolation of the prison as an enclave, separated from its surroundings by a perimeter wall. Foucault used this diagram of power to amplify his previous work on the medical gaze and the birth of the clinic as a place controlled by modern, specialized, scientific, rational knowledge. Clearly the isolated prison-machine was a potent and highly symbolic pacification device, a fragment with wide implications for the city.

Introduction: A Definition of Balkanization

Foucault distinguished between two types of enclaves, both of which he called "heterotopias." On the one hand were places of centralized, authoritarian, state control and violence (like prisons, clinics, hospitals, and military structures). On the other hand were the interstitial places of escape into highly specialized, often repressed, civilian worlds, where established values were inverted or disrupted (such as brothels, bathhouses, and markets). Both sets of places were distinct from other areas of society, but for very different reasons, as Benjamin Genocchio clarified in "Heterotopia and its Limits." (*Transition* 41 [1993]: 38–41). He described heterotopias of discipline or compensation because of the purity and rigidity of their enforcement of set norms and heterotopias of illusion because of their systematic disregard of the normative, societal rules in pursuit of pleasure and/or profit.

The process of Balkanization involves the creation of such guarded enclaves, sometimes located in the center of the city but often on the periphery, devoted either to maintenance of rigid order or to its subversion. The areas around and between such enclaves become zones of freedom, travel, and terror, where super-violent, free-fire anarchy might erupt at any moment. In the ensuing sociology of fear, the connective tissue and flows of urban life collapse into a system of rigid, militarized control, bloody warfare, and subterranean resistance. The Balkan model involves enclaves or fragments that act as ministates (surrogates for distant superpowers), declaring war on each other, invading each other, devastating each other's populations, and cutting each other's communication systems.

The Balkan model introduces a level of fragmentation and violence that we do not immediately associate with America. People still have water and electricity in most American cities. They do not live in basements and only emerge at night because of shelling and snipers as in Mostar, nor do they rely on the United Nations for their food as in Sarajevo. Sections of highway have not earned the designation "sniper alley."

Yet American cities have their own wastelands—by-products of a system of fragmentation that operated between the poles of Foucault's two extremes of heterotopia. Fragmentation had become the norm for nineteenth-century American cities, with their tradition of large state, commercial, and industrial institutions in separate enclaves, surrounded by segregated neighborhoods, and with zoning ordinances enforcing the various enclaves. Already in the 1920s, sociologists like Robert E. Park and Ernest Burgess in Chicago referred to American cities as "melting pots" in which different ethnic groups were segregated in tightly defined neighborhoods, meeting and intermingling at work and play, before moving on to the suburbs and further segregation. In *Good City Form* (MIT Press, 1984), Kevin Lynch illustrated a system diagram of a "city-machine" made of such mono-functional districts, neighborhoods, or discrete enclaves linked by segregated channels of high-speed transportation and communication. In this city-machine, an enclave could decay and be replaced by a new part in a different location without disrupting the balance of the overall system. Spiro Kostof in *The City Shaped* (Little, Brown, 1991) adapted this diagram of the city-machine to the radial distribution of new satellite towns around a central "mother" city. Kostof implied a Bentham-esque, Foucaultian, Panopticon-like power relationship between the center and edge of the garden city-region. In *Edge City: Life on the New Frontier* (Doubleday, 1991), Joel Garreau argued that such peripheral enclaves along the highways have an independent urban life of their own, while Peter Calthorpe in *The Next American Metropolis: Ecology, Community, and the American Dream* (Princeton Architectural Press, 1993) projected this enclave system (revised to be more ecologically responsible) into an optimistic, suburban future.

While this system of suburban fragmentation appears benign, even desirable, to many, critics of the postmodern city have adapted Foucault's analysis to study the carceral aspects of the cellular suburban system, leading to the Balkan analogy. Mike Davis, in *City of Quartz: Excavating the Future in Los Angeles* (Random House, 1992), pointed to the breakdown of relationships between neighborhoods in a city-machine like Los Angeles due to its segregation by class and race, as well as the armed perimeters formed around its residential communities, its gang turfs, and the privatized public realm of its shopping malls and central business district. In America, under the domination of the city-machine, distances between urban enclaves and neighborhoods have increased with the speed of the highways. Relationships between enclaves have become attenuated, as neighborhoods retreat behind defensive perimeters, relying on mechanical means to communicate. Relationships between parts of the city have been severed as roads and bridges have closed, collapsed, or never been built, and whole districts have been reduced to rubble. Travel between enclaves is dependent on the car and is controlled by the traffic police (like the high-tech L.A. Highway Patrol videotaped beating Rodney King). Davis was able to apply the rigid side of the heterotopic analysis to the enclave system of Los Angeles and to demonstrate a series of explosive tensions between the various fortified pockets of control. In this process of suburbanization the abandoned inner-city neighborhoods have been left to rot, becoming battlegrounds similar to those in Sarajevo. These interstitial areas were accelerated heterotopias of illusion with an especially violent edge.

The process of Balkanization may thus involve violence sponsored by the state or by surrogate ministates. It may also involve civilian violence against other civilians, with the state intervening, or civilian violence against the state, as in the L.A. riots. I would like to look more closely at the two categories of fragmentation and violence by the state and by civilians that correspond to Foucault's two heterotopias. Then I would like to examine the role of these spaces and the spectacle of simulated violence in the media, in what Evans perhaps would have termed a "pacification process."

The Balkan Model:
The City and State, Fragmentation and Violence

Foucault's emphasis on the violence of the state in his hetero-topias of compensation serves as a reminder of the perennial connection between the city, state, and Balkanization. Many cities have dual origins as armed camps and trading posts. Others were places of ritualized murder and sacrifice to the gods, later becoming places of public incarceration and execution. Cities have always been the focus of state power and violence. Medieval city walls provided freedom, privileges, and protection for ex-feudal inhabitants in city-states, but these walls also incarcerated the city within their rigid geometry, with specialized streets for traders and, later, ghettos for non-Christians. Subdivisions within the city were also frequent between warring clans and factions. Medieval Italian cities had many towers and fortified blocks belonging to rival groups. In accordance with Islamic law, medieval cities were created around cul-de-sacs, creating large, internally oriented island-blocks for clans or families, with the bare exterior walls of courtyard houses facing the street and neighboring cell structure. In ancient China, the army enforced wide avenues between large city blocks to ensure troop movements in times of trouble, long before Baron Hauss-mann's plans for Paris. Thus, the state-sponsored subdivision of the city into specialized enclaves has a long history, even before the Enlightenment and its acceleration in the Industrial Revolution. The advent of the modern nation-state clearly gave this process of Balkanization much greater power, urgency, and range even before the institutionalization of four segregated functions in Congrès Internationaux d'Architecture Moderne (CIAM) modernist manifestos.

Foucault highlighted the mono-culture of centralized, disciplined, ocular, state power, which has been a peculiarity of French government ever since the age of Louis XIV. For over a century in France centralized state power, not civilian market forces, has been the driving energy behind the classification and differentiation of communities (as in Prussia and Russia). This continental theory, based on Georg Hegel's schema, saw the state as a rational, moral force—the embodiment of Immanuel Kant's moral realm of noble duty. The state harnessed the market and the empirical realm of the senses, commerce, and desire in order to curb chaos, counter fragmentation, and advance the interests of modernization. State power sanctioned the use of violence to achieve such goals. Friedrich Nietzsche's superman's will-to-power, Vladimir Lenin's dictatorship of the proletariat, Vladimir Jablotinsky's Zionism, and Martin Heidegger's existential endorsements of Adolf Hitler's blood-and-soil racism could all be called into the service of radical, anti-democratic, accelerated exercises of state power. The tragic reality of the Balkans shows in detail the downside of this carceral model with its petty dictatorships and paramilitary gangs, thus illustrating the power and violence of the state within small enclaves.

Such small-scale demonstrations of state power and violence are not restricted to Sarajevo. At a larger scale the Berlin Wall and the Green Line in Beirut are recent examples of disjunctions that cut across historical fabric. In metropolitan London the Irish Republican Army has exploded bombs throughout the city in a multiyear campaign that has closed down many public facilities, varying from department stores and railway stations to post offices and pubs. The financial district is now like an armed camp with restricted vehicular access, security checks, and surveillance cameras at special entry gates. Even with the recent cease-fire, the city fathers have decided to keep the new gates. As in the so-called "no go" areas in Belfast, the British Army and Metropolitan Police are perpetually on guard, establishing a security perimeter around a valuable enclave of global finance. Within the enclave, further security layers guard individual office blocks, while the electronic channels of global communication contain additional security codes.

In America it is the apparent absence and clandestine nature of state power that is remarkable, encouraging conspiracy theories. But American history has its own share of state-sponsored violence. Robert Goodman in *After The Planners* (Simon and Schuster, 1972) viewed the inner-city, federal, urban renewal programs in the 1960s as exercises in state violence in an American tradition stretching back to the relocation of Native American tribes to western reservations. The Federal Bureau of Investigation's violent eradication of the Black Panthers clearly represented a far wider abuse of state power under J. Edgar Hoover's directorship (honed in the anti-Communist Eugene McCarthy period). In the 1980s documented revelations surrounding the William Casey Central Intelligence Agency, the Iran-Contra and Bank of Credit and Commerce International (BCCI) scandals and the FBI's persecution of the Committee in Solidarity with the People of El Salvador (CISPES) have confirmed the long-suspected clandestine connection between guns, drug cartels, and American foreign and domestic policy. These revelations and the American abduction of and court case against General Manuel Noriega of Panama, with its ensuing disclosures about CIA activities and drug cartels in the U.S. and South America, reinforced a ghastly impression of secret state participation in the creation of the American ghettos as marketplaces and sale points for the drug cartels. For conspiracy buffs, even the bombing of the financial enclave of the World Trade Center in downtown New York had its connections to state agencies. The "blow-back" of CIA-trained Afghani rebels (partially financed through the rebels' control of the opium fields) formed the core of the accused bombers. In addition, the FBI employed an Egyptian counter-intelligence agent to spy on the conspirators. The bombing also revealed that the elite U.S. Presidential Guard Corps had its New York headquarters in the same building using the same garage.

The Balkan Model:
Civilian Violence and Fragmentation

Foucault noted, in addition to the enclaves of state discipline and violence, areas of slippage and freedom, the heterotopias of illusion, where social norms and conventions were disrupted, inverted, and distorted. These areas were closely defined pockets of relative anarchy—mirror images of the Panopticon. Foucault's analysis reversed a long German tradition of revulsion against the rationalized industrial city, with its ceaseless dynamic. This disturbing, alienating dynamic was precisely that ascribed by Hegel to bourgeois, civil society in the cities (which had to be checked by the state bureaucracy and the rural-based nobility). The Germanic tradition continued from Goethe's *Faust* to the pioneering sociology of Ferdinand Tönnies and Georg Simmel (reflecting Germany's late and rapid industrialization), and ended up as a conservative strand of both Hitler and Heidegger. In this shocked view the free-wheeling, urban dynamic had to be contained; otherwise truth, work, and use would become irrelevant in the free play of disjunctive heterotopic space. It was this freedom that made this space valuable to Foucault, in opposition to the restraint of the prison. Everything in these spaces floats with no fixed value, like a commodity. Urban enclaves such as marketplaces, department stores, and malls feed on this frenzy of uncertainty, promoting a sense of modernity, insecurity, and shock. As in Antonin Artaud's Theater of the Absurd and Jean Genet's play, *The Balcony* (set in a brothel during a revolution), the shock of the new releases the urban imagination into a realm where roles are reversed, genders switched, and fantasy and reality are interchanged.

Cities have long contained such zones of freedom as engines for their development. The simultaneous presence of highly disparate objects, activities, peoples, spaces, and buildings has been one of the characteristics of the free market model of capitalist urban development for the past 200 years. Ever since the advent of the Industrial Revolution in the 1780s, free market economists have argued for the violent, anarchic, economic model in which all regulations are suspended—the equivalent of the contemporary British and Polish economic shock therapy. Richard Sennett in *The Uses of Disorder: Personal Identity and City Life* (Knopf, 1970) explored some of the social aspects of this form of heterotopia, in which each citizen has an equal right to articulate his or her wishes to the anarchic maximum. Jane Jacobs has documented the historic role of cities as pioneering economic engines of growth in *Cities and the Wealth of Nations: Principles of Economic Life* (Random House, 1984) and *The Economy of Cities* (Random House, 1969). Such urban enclaves of commercial privilege formed the social basis of the free city-states of the Renaissance and the mercantile city-states (such as London, Geneva, and Amsterdam) of the Enlightenment. In the form of Hong Kong and Singapore, such cities are still at work today as enclaves of hyper-development.

The rhetorical potential of such heterotopic enclaves for poetic, surreal juxtapositions was beautifully illustrated in Rem

Koolhaas's *Delirious New York: A Retroactive Manifesto for Manhattan* (Oxford University Press, 1978). Koolhaas demonstrated in urban terms how each cell in the city's grid could be programmed floor by floor in a vertical mosaic of skyscraper enclaves, creating a dream world of incredible diversity and density. His study highlighted the power of great capitalist corporations, such as John D. Rockefeller's Standard Oil monopoly, in the creation of superblock urban enclaves on a vast new scale. Such giant enclaves within the city-machine would compete with each other for economic advantage to the benefit of all—especially large—corporations. Zoning experiments along these free market, deregulated, hyper-developmental enclave lines proposed by Peter Hall in England produced the Thatcherite Docklands Enterprise Zone of the 1980s. The intention was to unleash the flow of free market capital in this depressed inner-city area. Similar zones have been proposed as part of American urban renewal packages by recent administrations.

The illusory and speculative nature of such free market enclaves might be illustrated by their frequent need of rescue by the state. Robert Fitch in *The Assassination of New York* (Verso, 1993) maintained that the Rockefellers, despite their great wealth, were hamstrung by the half-empty Rockefeller Center through the depression of the 1930s. According to Fitch, the Rockefellers were only able to make good on their investment by persuading the city to build a subway line to Rockefeller Center and to condemn cheaper properties on 7th and 8th avenues, before they sold out to Japanese interests in the late 1980s. A similar history of state rescue may be found in London's Canary Wharf Project, which went bankrupt and is only forty percent occupied ten years after completion (just as the twin towers of the World Trade Center stood empty until filled with state offices in the late seventies). In London remedial state interventions and infrastructure costs since the unplanned free market experiment began have been set at around $1.2 billion, with the Jubilee Tube Line expected to add another $1.5 billion. All of this is quite modest compared to the $500 billion debt left to the U.S. taxpayers by the executives of the deregulated American savings and loan industry, who so precipitously rebuilt the American skyline with empty skyscrapers (see Joel W. Barna,

The See-Through Years: Creation and Destruction in Texas Architecture 1981–1991 [Rice University, 1992]).

The wasted resources in such failed enclaves of hyper-development have been inevitably contrasted with enclaves of disinvestment and poverty in global cities like Hong Kong, Singapore, New York, London, and Tokyo. These cities contain and exploit blatant incquities and imbalances between areas of hyper-investment and of abject poverty and disinvestment. We are all familiar with the contrast between the boat people of Hong Kong and Norman Foster's Hong Kong and Shanghai Bank tower, a beacon of the global financial market. Parallel contrasts in America might include the building of office towers in downtown Los Angeles and New York as both cities lost 300,000 industrial jobs and received over a million new immigrants from the southern United States and Latin America. Given such imbalances, it is not surprising that such cities have throughout history had high crime rates, active police forces, and prominent prisons.

The American experience of this social polarization has been different for a number of reasons. The federally financed mass flight of the middle class to the suburbs left only the wealthy and poor, polarized by race, in the central cities. Perhaps because of the cold war, the state never really intervened to mediate the inner-city situation, despite the wars on poverty and welfare programs. As a result America suffered a spectacular series of urban insurrections during the seventies and eighties, culminating in the 1992 riots in Los Angeles. This remarkable absence of the state (except at the times of riots) combined with the extraordinary absence of gun control has allowed American civilian violence to reach unprecedented levels in small enclaves, inspiring the Balkan analogy.

Heterotopic freedom in this case has been interpreted by the National Rifle Association and weapons manufacturers as the constitutional right to bear firearms. These interested parties have long campaigned to make this armed image of freedom as American as apple pie. No one protested as scared suburbanites, white supremacists, religious fanatics, and old-style mobsters exercised their constitutional right to buy automatic weapons. Nor did many people object when gang members slaughtered one other, even carrying their weapons into school (teenage murder rates increased by 95% between 1984 and 1992 under the "get tough" Ronald Reagan-George Bush crime campaigns). Only with the arrival of a fragile peace amongst inner-city gangs and the enormous wealth and firepower of the South American drug cartels has handgun control become a political possibility in America.

Despite the official mythology of freedom and the lone, aberrant gunman, the risk of violent crime in America is clearly linked to poverty, class, race, age, gender, and even zip code. Market analysts and politicians have long understood this phenomenon and used it to their advantage. Michael J. Weiss in *The Clustering of America* (Harper and Row, 1989) used postal zip codes, market sales information, and U.S. Census Bureau statistics to identify micro-neighborhoods (classified into forty socioeconomic profiles) scattered across the nation. It is easy to track the enclaves of disinvestment where the vast majority of violent crime is concentrated. In California teenage Latinos make up 35% of the population, but they account for 60% of the murders and their victims are predominantly Latinos or blacks. In New York, the rate of incarceration of black male youths is higher than that of black male youths under apartheid in South Africa.

These enclaves of disinvestment reverse normal codes of controlled development; they are pockets of free-fall, urban implosion, partaking of a frenzied violence far beyond Foucault's heterotopia of illusion with its brothels and bathhouses. This urban hyper-violence is matched only by the half-machine cyborgs of the *Robocop* science-fantasy movies. Here the police plead for their own automatic weapons, claiming sometimes to be outgunned by teenage gangs. Organized violence by drug-related gangs has reduced these areas to rubble and suffering, parallel to the destruction perpetuated by the paramilitary gangs of Balkan ministates. In America the taboo against state intervention in the gun market also appears to extend to the drug and sex markets of the inner city, where many deinstitutionalized mental patients, single mothers, and homeless people have been dumped in city- and state-owned hostels to form what Camilo Vergara has called "The New American Ghetto" (see "Our Fortified Ghettos" *The Nation* 258 [January 1994]: 124).

The Balkan Analogy: Media and the Pacification of the City

In *Forget Foucault* (Semiotext(e), 1987) Jean Baudrillard argued that Foucault's models of the gaze, ocular inspection, discipline, and punishment; his patterns of scientific power, domination, and resistance; and his models of the body, sexuality, and desire were all obsolete. Foucault's ability to speak logically of such topics marked their death and disappearance as live issues. For Baudrillard the media was producing a world in which it was impossible to differentiate between the real, the simulation, the simulacra, and the fake. Fantasy, fiction, advertising, reenacted events and real-time reporting merged into a new form of animated, composite, urban imagination. This new urban consciousness was available everywhere and it affected everyone's perception of the city. In such an accelerated hyper-space Foucault's heterotopia of illusion appeared as a frozen, fictional precursor, as did the calm fantasy of the 360-degree perspectival space of Bentham's central jailer in the Panopticon. In this phantasmagoria of media images, the spectacle of urban violence and mayhem took its place alongside a National Geographic special on rain forest pygmies or a reenactment of Civil War battles.

While the media exploit a violent image of the inner city for countless, very popular, cop shows, their general emphasis is on the role of fate and the lone killer—the Lee Harvey Oswald syndrome. There were, for instance, three television specials (one on each major network) on the life of Amy Fisher, a suburban Long Island teenager who shot her lover's wife. Mass murders involving the violent slaughter of four or more people dominate the headlines, playing on Americans' insecurities, although such crimes represent a tiny proportion of the national epidemic of homicides. Dismissed postal workers, ex-students, deranged family men, and aggrieved immigrants are liable to wreck havoc with random fire into restaurants, Wal-Mart parking lots, places of employment, commuter trains, and even university campuses, stockbrokers' offices, and judges' chambers. No one is safe, so it is hardly surprising that people are scared to leave their homes, even in the suburbs.

Spectacles of real and simulated aestheticized violence scare, and at the same time, anaesthetize the urban population. These narratives present a shocking array of images, a visual equivalent of aphasia, far more compressed and accelerated than the life of the city feared by Hegel and his successors. In such German theories shock created a numbing effect, leading to a reduced perception of reality, a closing down of consciousness, and the blocking out of once communal activities. Sigmund Freud argued that the stronger the stimulus or shock (especially in the modern city), the stronger the screen erected in defense. Following this logic, the urban hyper-violence of television shows would lead to enormous psychological blocks erected against a real experience of the city. Reciprocal interaction would always be feared and regulated; standardized, reduced experiences *a la* Disney would be preferred. It is not difficult to see how such violent propaganda in the media would serve to support the Balkanization of the city into safe enclaves of hyper-investment where high security would produce high returns, high rents, and increased values for owners and merchants alike (a similar line of argument would support the division of Europe into nation-states). Nor is it difficult to see how spectators whose spirits had been numbed by endless scenes of senseless urban violence would prefer the tastefully aestheticized, protected, urban simulacra (theme parks) to what they had been told of the "real" thing.

Critics of Freud have argued that human beings (unlike other animals) learn at an early age to distinguish between reality and symbol, and between real self and image in the mirror. It would follow that humans are able to distinguish between mediated, symbolic hyper-reality and normal everyday lived reality, which has become ever more bureaucratized and controlled. The media's preoccupation with hyper-violence can be seen as compensation for this new state-enforced peacefulness, just as the fragmentary replication of the city in intense enclaves compensates for the acres of suburban sprawl. An odd, collective form of transference appears to make these novel compensatory simulacra and violent media images somehow satisfy our need for memory, change, and community, transforming these needs into profitable commercial transactions for cable television suppliers and mall operators.

Conclusion: The Limits of the Balkan Analogy

Hyper-violence and fragmentation in the Balkans and in American cities may thus be seen as a part of a pacification process if the media is considered as a closed loop, continually rerunning collective dream images of the ruins of the city, cutting inhabitants off from past communal values, interpersonal interactions, and wider experiences outside of safe havens. Despite Baudrillard's advice in *Forget Foucault*, it might be argued that the media represent the ultimate heterotopia of illusion, a vastly accelerated space of disjunctive occurrences and images. The fascinating display of visual and material fragmentation overlaid on the system of enclaves of the city-machine provides a constant spectacle with its own evolving internal dynamic, a constant distraction, and a potent means of pacification, far more effective than Bentham's central jailer. The media regulate the day of the commuter, while for the couch potato they create an illusion of a private, peaceful place with violence held at bay.

Baudrillard argued that Foucault never understood this new force, but I think that Robin Evans's last lectures promised a synoptic interpretation of how this dispersed and mediated system of fragments and enclaves worked as a system of total control and inspection, parallel in some ways to Bentham's jail. My intuition at the lectures was confirmed by the program of a memorial conference, which contained a diagram, drawn by Evans, of the system of communication and vision in postmodern architecture as a self-reinforcing, closed, conceptual loop. This loop (a triangle between imagination, the scopic regime of perspective, and three-dimensional architectural drawing conventions) provided a perfect means of control—a self-correcting means of stabilization and pacification of the physical, built environment despite its aesthetics of a shattered, dynamic diversity.

D. G. Shane is an architect, writer, and adjunct professor of architecture at Columbia University; he lectures at The Cooper Union and the University of Pennsylvania.

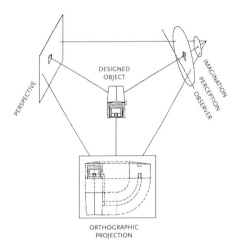

PERSPECTIVE

DESIGNED
OBJECT

IMAGINATION
PERCEPTION
OBSERVER

ORTHOGRAPHIC
PROJECTION

Drawing by Robin Evans, used in the brochure at his memorial service

Fear Not…

Mark Wigley interviewed by Peter Lang

PL: What brings me to the subject of the mortal city is a concern about the way popular views of the city have changed. We have gone from fearing the death of the city to fearing the city of death, and I think this is a very traumatic change. What are your feelings about the evolution in attitudes towards the city? Do you think the city is still salvageable?

MW: It is a difficult question because we live in the myth—and I think it is really a myth—that we once understood what a city was. But we know that the physical form of the city is radically changing all the time; one can almost look out of the window and see the city changing. We also know that people's relationships to the city change and, therefore, they change. That brings up the issue of who is the "we" that defines the city, because, typically, we have associated cities with large numbers of people. So when you deal with the question of death in the city or the death of the city, I guess those issues of definition are, for me, impossible to separate.

PL: Can we understand perceptions of fear and violence within the physical context of the city?

MW: Again, I think the tricky part of the question is that if we associate cities with buildings, with physical objects, and so on,

Newark, New Jersey

what we are really pointing to is a "residue" of an older idea of what a city is. Buildings are mechanisms of representation—systems of organizing things—and, in that sense, they are political constructions. What we now know is that the boundaries of a city no longer coincide with its physical limits. To some extent our real public space now is in the media.

I am not sure I would accept that there is any more or any less violence in the streets today than there was in the past. It is true that our relationship to the violence has changed—you referred to "fear"—but it may have to do with the fact that space is no longer clearly defined in our minds. The uncertainty about a definition of the city is an uncertainty about what space can be occupied and what space cannot. If we cannot define the space in which we feel we can operate, we are already exposing ourselves to the random violence that we see in the streets.

We believe the streets are violent not because we are in the streets experiencing that violence, but because we see the violence on television. Likewise, the perception is that there is now much more violence inside the home than ever before when it is much more likely to be true that the endless violence of the home is now becoming more visible. Why is it becoming visible? Because the boundaries of the home are no longer clear; because the media, exactly the same media that has confused our idea of what a city is, has confused our idea of what a home is. On both sides, we have the conception that there is more violence.

PL: What adds to the confusion is that there seem to be different types of violence occurring at the same time. For example, in Sarajevo there is a siege mentality, which is archaic in its form; yet, in Los Angeles there is an imploding city. The confusion that is generated from having such a conflict of experiences makes me wonder whether we can more clearly understand the siege mentality than we can the imploding city.

MW: Well, that is interesting because you could say that both of these very visible and horrific struggles are attempts to maintain an old spatial order. In the case of Bosnia-Herzegovina, it is fairly obvious. The different groups are defending traditional spaces—either religious or physical—and, in fact, what they are insisting on is that these two things should be the same. So there is a desperate attempt to make the political order, as it were, coincide with the spatial order. I think you can say the same of Los Angeles. The struggle is not over who controls which piece of territory, but rather who defines what constitutes territory.

PL: What I see in this is that there are two paradigms. Let us take Paris in 1968. There were barricades—people protecting their territory from the outside and flushing out the unwanted elements. Then there was this phenomena in Los Angeles, where you have the destruction of one's own terrain, which I find, again, a very ambiguous statement.

MW: I agree, but I would add that the particular phenomenon in Los Angeles is almost a perfect illustration of what I was saying. When it is clear what your space is, the one thing you never do is destroy it. But what if your struggle is not over who has the space but who determines what the space is? Then the most polemical way of making one's point is to destroy one's own space and this, for me, was a very articulate, systematic move. That is not to say there was a plan, but it was an absolutely understandable symptom of an urgent situation. What the people of Los Angeles were making clear is that they no longer have a sense of space and no amount of token property—which is in this case largely slum rental and over-mortgaged property—can provide this.

I think there is always an attempt to make no distinction between space and politics. If we were to start projecting global histories over millennia, we would find that at all the different historical sites, at any one time, there were constant attempts to maintain an identity between political, spatial, and psychic economies—keeping everything in sync, as it were. In theory, a building will be like the political structure that enabled it and sustained it and like the people that will inhabit it. But the very earnestness of these attempts betrays the fact that there is always considerable slippage between political, psychic, and physical structures. Each side is a specific renegotiation of what these structures are, a negotiation that is always being exceeded or defined by the forces it tries to regulate—sometimes catastrophically. The specific violence of Los Angeles has a lot to do with the specific collapse of very specific ideas of space. After all, we should not forget that Los Angeles, for some time now, has been the pet city of contemporary theorists who, for many years, have celebrated it as the perfect model of the loss of the previous spatial condition. Los Angeles has been long touted as the postmodern city, the stepping stone to *Bladerunner*.

At the same time, it is absolutely important to try and understand the relationship this specific struggle might have with the global scene because, if there is a generic rule, it is that violence is always placed into some kind of a conceptual ghetto. Our culture survives by believing that it has safely located violence in a particular space. It is very easy for us to think that violence can be located, for instance, in Los Angeles, New York, or Detroit. By placing it in these ghettos, we forget the much less visible violence that causes exponentially more destruction and deaths than these symbolic events. There is an ongoing daily violence of everyday life that is, in the end, not radically different from that scene in Los Angeles, but is never acknowledged as such. For example, many of the people who are so offended at the violence of Los Angeles are, in their own lives, participating in the cover-up of domestic violence, refusing to see any association between the two. We have to realize that blood flowing in the streets is only one symptom, and not necessarily a very significant one, of a structural phenomenon that organizes the whole political economy of our society. It may well be, as has been proven time and time again in history, that blood in the streets is nothing more than a tactical cover-up for a much more insidious, much more radically structural phenomenon.

To put it in the most obvious terms, there are still many people dying, every night, in the streets of Los Angeles. Those deaths—those less well-known, less romantic, less televisual events—are now ignored more than ever because they seem insignificant in comparison to what was so obviously a big media event—the whole city, as it were, on fire. That is the first level. The second level is the violence that never can be seen, even if we were to have a camera. This is the most intensely political violence of all, and architecture is completely complicit with this. I would go so far as to argue (since I favor conspiracy theories) that architecture is no more than the cover-up of violence.

PL: That brings up the question of what role architects see themselves playing in their vision of the future. We are familiar with certain social critiques—whether it is alienation in the modern society, the loss of a public life, or the invasion of electronic media—and we could discuss what has brought us to this level. If what you are saying is true, do you think that we have to completely revise our methods and start with a *tabula rasa* to build new structures of understanding?

MW: Well it has to be said that the danger in hyping an apparently new condition, like alienation, is that it enables us to envision some sense of a previous condition to which we would like to return. Every time somebody gets nostalgic, it leads to trouble. The very appeal to some idyllic condition before violence plays a major role in promoting the violence it appears to be rejecting. To cite the most obvious example, the right to carry guns in America is justified by a desire to preserve some questionable interpretation of the supposedly peaceful intentions of the "founding fathers," but the very idea that you have to protect this idyllic political ideal is responsible for enormous numbers of people being killed every day. The right to defend oneself against violence is responsible for the lethal availability of the weapons that effect that violence. Defense here is nothing but aggression.

I think this is also true of all those battalions of social theorists who claim that we have lost the wonderful public space we used to have, because it is not so clear there ever was such a space, and if there was, it was not so wonderful. By whom was it occupied? Was it men or women? Which class groups? Which structure was being preserved? In any case, a public square is just one technology of communication, which makes possible a communication to a certain number of people in a certain way and maintains a certain violent, political regime. So it makes no sense to say that, because we no longer have the public space that we used to have, we are falling into a condition of chaos, and that the nonspatial quality of the media has disturbed our previously secure environment of closed house leading to open public space. On the contrary, our previous ideas of house and public square were just certain technologies of communication—technologies that sustained specific regimes of overt and covert violence—at certain moments in time. The television, fax machine, and computer represent other modes of communication, other spaces that are, in their own way, just as clearly defined. But the transition from one to another is always brutal, as are the conditions within them.

PL: I also question the notion that the ideas of history involve an interplay between progress and nostalgia. I do think it is very important to try to understand what is nothing more than a romantic confusion.

MW: Yes, because, clearly, nostalgia is a lethal weapon and it kills people.

PL: I have the impression that "the American way"—which, in my opinion, is the perfection of the mass consumer culture—has had a chance to incubate in the United States for a certain amount of years, and has reached a cumulative moment. What I see also is that, without other ideological challenges, and with a global media system, it will soon become a universal language.

MW: It is true that Cable Network News has taken over where the Pope left off. CNN is a kind of mechanism for representing the globe, which is what the major religions did for a long time. But that global capacity is equally matched by an insistence on specialization and individuality. There is not one mass consumer audience receiving one phenomenon. In fact, the phenomenon of so-called mass culture is a phenomenon of increasing specialization and a huge industrial complex that sets itself up in order to cater to that specialization. A case in point is the number of battles going on in Europe at the moment as a result of attempts to define increasingly smaller regional units. Nation-states are getting smaller, not bigger.

PL: And yet you have McDonald's penetrating each and every one of those separate terrains.

MW: McDonald's does not pose a threat, in my view, because the desire to eat at McDonald's is a desire to eat this global food—to eat, as it were, a symbol of one's participation in the globe. To eat plastic is to be on the map, if not to be human. I think it is easy to see the consumer as being manipulated by a relentless economic and political force presumably coming from one direction and having one particular agenda. But if there are insidious phenomena at work in our cultural scene, of which there is no doubt, they are just as visible in specialist operations of the most minute kind, including academic research into the horrors of McDonald's.

PL: I do not really see "McDonaldization" or mass consumer society as a conspiracy—absolutely not. What I see is an expanding system, or non-system, which has been allowed to grow unchecked, in this age without secular, ideological opposition. In this context it is difficult to sing praises for what is still, basically, a laissez-faire economy that essentially prevents a lot of people from ever reaching the doors of this consumer society. There are a lot of important social issues standing on the sidelines.

MW: I have no doubt about that; it is without question that the so-called consumer society is a society of institutionalized poverty. However, one cannot simply point to a part of that economy and identify it as entirely responsible. What is more crucial is to understand the relationship between McDonald's and those operations of our society that we think are acting in the interests of a more egalitarian model.

It is particularly true in architecture that very little research is being done to question the operations of supposedly sound egalitarian political models. To really mobilize ourselves for a more egalitarian social and political economy would be to seriously rethink the relationship between architecture and the political. In my view that cannot be done without facing directly—in a scholarly, careful way to say the very least—the question of violence. In other words it is only when one can truly appreciate the violence of the most simple, most innocuous architectural gesture that one could start to send certain architectural practices in another direction.

I find myself naively optimistic because I think that architecture, for once, is being positioned as a fundamental question in critical discourse. People who want to talk about politics talk about architecture first; people who want to talk about sexual identity talk about architecture; people who want to talk about philosophy talk about architecture. At the same time, I am cynical and embittered about the hypocrisy that goes under the name of politics, or political theorizing, in architecture. To rethink politics in architectural terms we will have to change our sense of what constitutes the political. At the moment, we have a sense of politics as something independent of architecture— something with which architecture has been aligned, assisted, blocked, and interfered, but of a different order. This conveniently frees up the architect to work anywhere for anyone.

PL: Henri Lefevre mentioned, back in the seventies, that after the modernists lost grip of their social planning in the fifties the only site of future projections or imaginations occurred in science fiction. Science fiction provides us with some very frightening and very reactionary visions of what could be, but it seems that architects have abandoned political roles for purely aesthetic ones.

MW: Architecture is, by any statistical analysis, a trivial discipline, an insignificant issue in contemporary culture. But the *idea* of architecture is just the opposite. The sense of space that architects protect and use and see themselves as the guardians of is fundamental to our collective conscience. One of the reasons that architects are unable to mobilize themselves politically is precisely because they are allowed their trivial position in our culture—their presence within the university and their input in one or two percent of the built environment—on condition that they preserve a certain kind of distinction between physical form and political structure in order that the relationship between them can be renegotiated in daily transactions. Their real responsibility is not simply to build a certain kind of building that sustains a certain kind of politics. It is not even their responsibility to build politically insignificant buildings, to be the decorators of cities, for instance, if one assumes, as our culture does, that decoration is insignificant, which I do not. Rather, it is architects' responsibility to preserve a certain sense of what the political is by preserving a certain sense of what a building is.

What architects are bound to do now is to refuse that role and, in refusing, to transform architecture or recover suppressed aspects of its operations. People who are nostalgic about the old space of the public square or frightened by the new public space offered by the television set are refusing to recognize the deeper political function of the public square as a technology of communication and a political structure in that sense. They are preserving the idea that there is this opposition between technologies of representation, which are always political, and architectural space, and that, somehow, architecture comes either before or after politics. Either it monumentalizes a regime or makes space for it, imprisoning people.

PL: I would like to think about students of architecture and urban planning. What do you think about *Les medicins sans frontières* (Doctors Without Frontiers), who involve themselves in Third World conditions—about the really phenomenological experience of their métiers and why architects do not do anything similar. We are very much in need of this type of intervention. I wonder if we can provide some sort of basic beginnings for a much more conscientious approach to urbanism.

MW: The idea of architects without frontiers is a very complex idea because, in our culture, the architect is supposedly the person responsible for frontiers. It would seem that, in an age in which we can no longer clearly define frontiers or boundaries, there would be a lot of both theoretical and practical work for architects. On the one hand there is a need for people to work in these undefined areas to provide definition in a classical architectural sense. On the other hand there is a need to pay attention to the extent to which a lack of frontiers might be a fundamental condition of those parts of architecture that seem so straightforward. This raises a question. It may be that architects without frontiers do not simply leave the traditional, institutional elements of architectural practice to find other sites on which to build. It may be that they also allow the difficulty of defining frontiers to infect those traditional institutional practices. If it is the case that we live in a time in which the frontiers are no longer clear, then it is also true that the limits of what constitute architecture are no longer clear. There is a call to go to the heart of the institutions of architecture and really question the apparent confidence with which they define limits.

So I do think that there is a whole series of roles available to architects as mobile agents, but I am not sure they will be agents for the frontier anymore. This is just to very much agree with your question and to take it so seriously as to understand that even the limits of architecture are no longer feared. You do not need to leave traditional sites of practice behind to lose the sense of frontier. Just as the Third World is right here at home, the architectural discipline is not what it was, if it ever was.

Frankly, no one knows what architecture is; it is a radical confusion with an apparently solid front. If architects were to really expose their dilemmas about architecture, I think this would be a necessary part of a straightforward practical engagement with political issues. As long as we pretend we know what architecture is, we can go into the Bronx or Guatemala and act with confidence and, in so doing, export a kind of misplaced imperialist attitude.

Architecture is interesting because it is fragile, much more fragile than television, for example. Television is a very systematic, clearly defined space, which is why it offers so much security. A building, on the other hand, is radically unclear, as children, of course, know perfectly well. We train our students to not think like children; we train them to not see ghosts, to not imagine that the limits of a space are enigmatic and unclear. We give them the sense that architecture is a solid, stable institution and it is not, it just is not.

PL: We attempt to codify the irrational to some extent. It seems to me that we are shifting the terrain of violence from a physical terrain to the terrain of architecture as a practice itself, and we could open it as a battleground.

MW: I think it is safe to say that all violence is institutional, which does not simply mean that institutions act violently. There is a certain kind of systematic, repetitive violence, much of which we do not see, that we call an institution. What we allow ourselves to see are isolated, symbolic moments, and we allow ourselves to see them only in order to neglect the other scenes. For example, it could be argued that we are now allowing ourselves to see certain forms of child abuse precisely in order that the majority of child abuse is, in a way, protected.

PL: It seems we desire, in a subconscious way, to make violence a spectacle, whereas a codified logic and rules permit a certain violence to take place within the public domain, while masking the violence that lies on the periphery.

MW: To give an obvious example: I could not kill a mouse with a hammer—I just could not do it, I know—but I can set a mousetrap to do it for me. So, I am responsible for the mouse's death, but I will not allow myself to witness it. I will use a prosthetic extension of my body to carry out the death. When people sit at their television sets, watching people being killed in Los Angeles, they are killing them. There is no question about it. The television set is, for a person watching the riots in Los Angeles, what the mousetrap is for me. There was never, for a moment, the thought that what was being seen in Los Angeles was just the most visible, most spectacular demonstration of the structural violence that organizes the most quiet, little town in the backwater of Tennessee, where nobody has been killed for the last five years. And anyway, if you go to these small towns, people are being killed all the time. I think that is the condition of our culture. We are not suddenly brutal; we have not become brutal in the last five minutes; we are a brutal society at every level. Television is just the latest weapon, as is the seemingly innocent ranch house in which the television sits. Architects have blood on their hands whether they like it or not—blood that does not simply go away if you declare yourself a pacifist; blood that cannot, as it were, be designed away by some politically or ethically correct architecture. All that can be done is to take account of it, to take responsibility for architecture's complicity in the traumas from which it seems so removed. This simple acknowledgment may, in the end have a more profound effect than the grandest of designs.

Mark Wigley is a professor of history and theory of architecture at the School of Architecture at Princeton University. He is the author of Architecture of Deconstruction: Derrida's Haunt *(MIT Press) and editor of* Violence and Space, Assemblage 20 *(MIT Press).*

Fig. 5. This key for a now lost photograph shows the author with a group of colleagues. He was believed to be number 6. Recent evidence, however, indicates that he was number 14.

The Appendix
Peter Anders

The following is what remains of a manuscript found near a burnt-down house shortly after the riots in Los Angeles. They seem to be notes for an unpublished book by Robert Dalton, an obscure but influential historian of statistical phenomena. Their discovery coincides with the disappearance of this author, and they may have formed part of his last work.

The text appears to have been a study of violence and urban disruption as the evidence of an underlying structure. The author indicates a familiarity with recent developments in complexity science through his repeated reference to "attractors." These attractors are assumed to form the hidden structure beneath current urban crises. Note 11 makes a direct reference to this, and there are allusions to it in other notes.

The attractors apparently underlie the form of the city as well. The author describes large-scale artificial forms, like skylines, to be subject to the same laws as forms found in nature. However, the appendix does not provide conclusive evidence of a connection between these attractors and social behavior. The discovery of a main text might prove the point, although its apparently small size does not indicate a rigorous analysis of the subject. Note 18 seems to acknowledge this.

Curious sub-themes of the text appear to have been the role of personal choice and identity operating under the influence of these attractors. Note 20 seems to refer to a crisis of personal responsibility—that crime is a result of nature not nurture. More than that, it seems to operate beyond the actual scale of the individual. This appears to be elaborated in note 21.

Other parts of the appendix, particularly note 17, allude to this negation of responsibility. We can only imagine the logic used here—or the consequences. Would these structures be the ultimate license for crime? Is all creative activity merely residue left in the wake of an attractor? Is this also true of inaction? These questions may never be answered . . . perhaps they should not be.

References to outside texts have been verified; however, some throw doubt on whether the main text ever existed. How, for instance, are we to understand note 35? How would the work to which note 25 refers have any relevance to the present subject? These and other questions would be resolved by the discovery of the main text, if indeed there is one to be found.

Illusion of Crisis

1.　　p. 2　　. . . forever immanent apocalypse.
"The end of the world" is a constant theme in our culture. Often qualified by "as we now know it," the concept is still the same. It indicates both a position of self-pity and of self-aggrandizement. It mourns the passing of better times, while placing us at the brink of Armageddon. Since no one can claim to have seen the beginning, at least we can be witnesses to the end.

2.　　p. 5　　Decay and emergence . . .
Ilya Prigogine's excellent study, *From Being to Becoming* (San Francisco: W. H. Freeman, 1980) discusses the values placed upon certain words like "decay." He claims that the process of decay is vital to the emergence of future orders. It clears the field and nourishes the new. Prigogine describes the instability of states as the hallmark of living systems. Death, in this case, is the ultimate stable state.

3.　　p. 7　　. . . with dry eyes.
Several years ago, an article by a renowned architectural critic mourned the death of New York. This position was based upon a fixed image of New York. Any deviation from this was regarded as evidence for his case. Cities, however, are dynamic systems, and expectations that things will remain in place will be disappointed. If the process is viewed without prejudice, decay can indicate the emergence of alternative orders.

4.　　p. 8　　"If this could solve danger."
Jane Jacobs, *The Death and Life of Great American Cities* (New York: Random House, 1961), 32.

5.　　p. 12　　Popular media's lugubrious . . .
Our awareness of civil unrest and urban violence is tied directly to the media's

portrayal of it in the daily news. We are confronted regularly with accounts of sensational crimes. On slow nights, the local news will feature crimes from other parts of the country. The apparent anarchy depicted is rarely analyzed for root causes.

6.   p. 13   ... an acquired taste.

American fascination with these subjects is a cultural phenomenon. If the great theme of European culture is love and death, the American counterpart would have to be sex and violence. They are the real-time equivalents of eternal values.

Structures of Attraction

7.   p. 15   ... movement of tectonic plates.

Statistics of crime usually do not reveal its causes. Incidents of crime, like volcanic activity, might indicate larger-scale movements, which cannot be understood without a substantial database and analysis. Although acts of violence are largely context specific, they reflect larger structural dynamics within the society.

8.   p. 17   "The cruel game of social life ... "

Georges Bataille, *Visions of Excess: Selected Writings 1927–1939*, edited and with an introduction by Allan Stoekl, translated by Stoekl with Carl R. Lovitt and Donald M. Leslie, Jr. (Minneapolis: University of Minnesota Press, 1985), 126. Bataille's Marxist stance toward the political structure of economics now seems dated. However, his proposal that the tribal rites of potlatch underlie the structure of economy still is unchallenged. The unrequited gift, in this case, is an admission of the recipient's inferiority, a loss of face. If this condition is socially reinforced, the situation of the recipient becomes intolerable. Violence against the donor/oppressor is one of the few options left available.

9.   p. 19   The withdrawal of the suppresser ...

Recent evidence of this is the carnage affecting the former Yugoslavia, Romania, Albania, and the former Soviet Union. Once the overbearing presence of the presiding government has been removed, the tribal constituents of the nations struggle to establish tribal nationalism. This is a restoration of governmental order along blood lines. Tribal memories of past transgressions seem, if anything, enhanced by the enforced delay in retribution.

10.   p. 25   "... evidence may always be decayed."

Nold Egenter, *Architectural Anthropology* Research Series 1 (Lausanne: Structura Mundi, 1991), 129.

11.   p. 31   The underlying form describes ...

The order hidden within an apparently disordered system is described as a "strange attractor." These structures are found in dynamic systems that have gone far beyond equilibrium. This concept may be applied both to living as well as inorganic systems. Cities exhibit many of the features of dynamic systems and, so, may possess attractors of their own.

12.   p. 40   Ritual and repetitive ...

Dr. Gottfried Meyer-Kress has suggested to me that fashion may be dictated by an attractor. The speed with which an idea or style is disseminated within a community indicates more about a hidden dynamic within the culture than the strength of the concept. This throws into question the role of artists in the culture. Are they authors of their work or merely evidence of the attractor?

13.   p. 40   With certain exceptions ...

Here I am referring to Tomás Valena's excellent study, *Stadt und Topographie* (Berlin: Ernst and Sohn, 1990). In it he and his students examined dozens of European cities in an effort to find the link between the development and structure of the city and underlying geological strata. Manhattan's skyline, for example, is partially due to the proximity of load-bearing schist to the surface.

14. p. 42   Both physical and social disruptions...
Self-similarity at a range of scales is known as "fractality." In the case of Manhattan's skyline, fractal units roughly shaped as rectilinear solids make up the city's overall form. The recurrence of this form at all scales, ranging from discarded packaging to the tallest skyscrapers, recalls natural formations in plants and geology.

15. p. 46   Context-driven decisions in...
The vast range of scale of U.S. governmental structure provides ample opportunity for inconsistency and contradiction. Perhaps we can only be grateful for this. A truly ordered and predictable government would inevitably be subject to error. However, the damage would be far greater. We need only look back to the 1930s for proof of this.

The Stability of Crisis

16. p. 52   "However, reason does not rule this world..."
Jacobs, *Death and Life*, 220.

17. p. 54   Mandelbrot dies exactly...
Naturally fractal forms are shapes resulting from chaotic forces acting on matter. This may be the result of forces external to the object, like wind upon rock formations, or internal, like cell growth within an organism.

18. p. 75   ...recurrence of patterns at different scales.
This also relates to fractality in dynamic systems. If the form of a city is an artifact of the society that produced it, perhaps the dynamics of that society can be described fractally as well. The attractors operating within a societal context would be difficult to assess. Presently the variables in operation are far too numerous to contemplate, let alone compile.

19. p. 79   "On the other... and blood going everywhere."
From an interview with a member of SPK. *Industrial Culture Handbook*, ReSearch 6/7 (San Francisco: ReSearch Publications, 1983), 101.

20. p. 85   If the larger structure reflects the smaller...
This is not a causal argument. Issues of personal responsibility enter here in ways that this study cannot answer. However, the criminal is part of his society and so is subject to its higher order. Whether that order is consciously generated or the result of turbulence in the system does not matter. Both would indicate the presence of an attractor.

21. p. 90   ...identity being a scale-related issue.
Stanislaw Lem has noted that a signature is dependent upon the distance from which it is viewed. At arm's length the signature is legible. From across the room, it is a meaningless scrawl. Through a microscope, it is a blur of ink and paper fibers.

22. p. 93   These self-regulating disasters...
Per Bak of the Brookhaven National Laboratory proposed that the nature of dynamic systems causes them to build up to a point of criticality. This highly

unstable point would be very sensitive to perturbation. The degree of response to the same stimulus varies. Bak performed several experiments with an unstable sand pile. Sand was added one grain at a time to a pile that had been built to a critical height. Avalanches of various sizes were produced with the same stimulus. In this way, the sand pile grew despite the avalanches, which essentially widened the base of the pile. As Roger Lewin states in his book, *Complexity* ([New York: Macmillan, 1992], 61) "And the avalanches of all size ranges . . . represent the power law distribution of response: The signature of a system that has got itself to a critical state."

23.   p. 94   . . . gentle collapse.
And, by extension, crisis is proof of the system's vitality.

The Transparent Structure of Entropy

24.   p. 102   . . . development of current economies.
In *The Wheels of Commerce* (vol. 2 of *Civilization and Capitalism 1500–1800*, trans. Reynolds Sian [Berkeley: University of California Press, 1992], 465) Fernand Braudel describes societal structure as a "set of sets": "The hierarchical order is never simple. All societies are diversified pluralities. They are divided against themselves and such division is probably intrinsic to their nature." This internal division into interest groups is as true today as it was for the medieval societies Braudel was describing. These groups maintain alliances as long as they benefit them. In times of crisis, the bonds may break. However, the individual groups may recombine into new sets.

25.   p. 107   "The index . . . "
J. G. Ballard, *War Fever* (New York: Farrar Strauss Giroux, 1990), 171–174.

26.   p. 112   The ready acknowledgment of politicians . . .
Tensions between special interest groups are often resolved poorly by government officials. Rather than appealing to a higher common interest, politicians often feel forced to advocate the position of the most powerful lobby. This enhances the power of that lobby at the expense of the society and forces a crisis between the groups. Resulting imbalances in representation are sometimes righted by actions outside the government, sometimes by actions outside the law.

27.   p. 123   The recently intensified . . .
The emergence of special interest lobbies over the past thirty years indicates a restructuring of society along new lines. Compared with earlier times, the model for society is no longer based upon a shared ideal of the future. Instead it aims to correct injustices, advocate the powerless, and enforce rights. Problems arise, however, when the correction, advocacy, and enforcement are not aligned with the ideals of other groups.

28.   p. 125   . . . a search for identity.
This is presaged by the development of postwar suburbs. While the concept of suburban communities has its roots in the nineteenth century, it finds its fullest expression in the United States in the 1950s.

29.   p. 132   The centripetal development . . .
Here I should note efforts made by Robert E. Park, Ernest Burgess, and the Chicago School at describing the dynamics of urban decentralization. It is interesting to note that this work was done at the same time that Frank Lloyd Wright was proposing his ideal decentralized city, Broadacre.

30.   p. 135   "The slurbs . . . contributed to the architecture of entropy."
Robert Smithson, "Entropy and the New Monuments," *The Writings of Robert Smithson* (New York: New York University Press, 1979), 11.
31.   p. 141   . . . resulting from these introductions.
The development of transportation and communications technologies has been followed closely by urban decentralization. Invention, in this case, assists in overcoming distance. Whereas the forces that drove the suburban developments were automobiles and telephones, the current forces are computers and television.
32.   p. 154   "It divides the territories . . ."
Eliel Saarinen, *The City: Its Growth, Its Decay, Its Future* (Cambridge, MA: MIT Press, 1943) 270.
Although they both used the term "organic decentralization," Wright and Saarinen intended mutually opposing results. Saarinen's work in city planning held to a cellular-based pattern. His plans broke the concentrated city into smaller fragments, each of which maintained the density of the original. Wright's strategy decreased density, the ideal being an individual unit on a private acreage. Wright's model, for better or worse, prevailed in the postwar construction of suburbs.
33.   p. 168   The increased reports of violence . . .
This, in turn, accelerates the flight from the urban center. The exodus depletes the tax base, which reduces the city services to the needy. One can see the dynamics of this cycle repeating itself until all those with the means escape the city entirely. This overly simplified scenario demonstrates the logic of attractors operating in a social setting.

Social Recombinance
34.   p. 175   The attractor driving the . . .
The same phone that lets us speak with a former neighbor in the city allows us to speak with a colleague in Europe. The car used for commuting allows visits to friends hundreds of miles away. In this way, changes within the city do not necessarily indicate social collapse. Perhaps scales of distance between citizens create the illusion of dissipation when, in fact, larger more transparent orders are emerging.
35.   p. 182   A link between the smaller . . .
In this way the citizen is like a footnote in a text. He is dependent upon the main text, his community, for validity. In turn, he refers to the world beyond to validate the text.
36.   p. 195   . . . to counteract the entropy.
The crisis of identity, both for individuals and for groups, is evident in many new social institutions. The absence of a tangible community has led to the success of shopping malls. Theme parks offer narrative meaning to public gatherings, perhaps vestigial of religious pilgrimages and events. Computerized bulletin board services give users opportunities to try on various identities within their electronic gathering spaces.
37.   p. 202   . . . dangers of a radical passivity.
An understanding of the attractors governing these phenomena presents this dilemma. Any attempt to act on the basis of judgment is subject to the attractor's

influence. The same is true of the decision not to act. An attempt to maintain an order may stall the creation of a newer order.

38.   p. 214   ... creation or decay.
Seen without the passage of time, they are indistinguishable.

39.   p. 220   The beginning...
Robert Smithson, "Proposal 1972," *The Writings of Robert Smithson* (New York: New York University Press, 1979), 221.

Peter Anders is an architect and teaches at the School of Architecture at the New Jersey Institute of Technology.

El Niño and the Rhino

Masse

Translated from the French by
Anne-Sophie Cerisola

El Niño has been spotted out at sea. It won't be long now.

Already?!

What do you mean "already"? This isn't unusual... it's just going to be El Niño's season, that's all...

Again?!

What do you mean "again"? There are these seasons every year. They're always the same...

Always?!

What do you mean "always"? Of course not. El Niño's season is *his* season—it's he who decides every five years...

All by himself?!

Obviously, he can do what he wants with his season. He's an adult even though he's still a child...

And why is this El Niño's season? Did you see what he did last time with his season. Do you really think this was adult and responsible?

EL NIÑO AND THE RHINO

MASSE

93

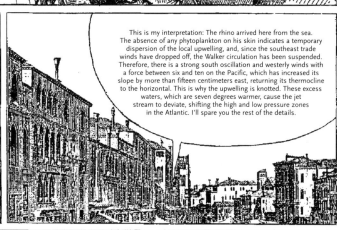

EL NIÑO AND THE RHINO

MASSE

Although thousands of Angelenos remained at least temporarily out of work Thursday, some labor experts predicted that Monday's devastating earthquake would ultimately cost fewer jobs than the 30,000 lost after the 1992 Los Angeles riots.

Still, state officials said they are preparing for a surge in unemployment insurance claims from workers displaced by the magnitude 6.6 temblor. Since Monday, insurance claims at some state Employment Development Department offices in the San Fernando, Santa Clarita and Antelope valleys have been running up to 30% higher than usual.

One of those in line at the Canoga Park unemployment office Thursday was Julianna Stevenson, 5

The Case for Letting Malibu Burn and Slide

Diane Ghirardo

To those who live elsewhere, the events in Los Angeles since April 1992 are but an eerie fulfillment of biblical prophecies about the wages of decadence and self-indulgence. Each successive convulsion—from urban uprising to fire, to earthquake, to mud flows—was magnified by the marvels of media technology, as continuous feeds satiated sensibilities and airwaves around the globe. However, sympathy for the victims should not obscure crude facts: Much of Los Angeles lives in obstinate defiance of the region's geography and ecology.

It gives one pause to reflect on the fact that during the past two decades far more devastating disasters have occurred in Iran, Armenia, India, Croatia and Bosnia-Herzegovina, but none of these received a comparable avalanche of attention. Why this is so has much to do with the massive media presence in Los Angeles, but even more with the image of southern California as a place of decadence, mystery, luxury, and danger. Indeed, the homes of many famous film and rock stars perished during the recent quakes, slides, and fires.

From outside, L.A.'s four major disasters seem related only in terms of location, but appearances are deceptive. The deep matrix of exploitation that binds them together transcends the obvious distinctions between natural disasters and social uprising. More to the point, the grinding fate of millions of exploited

Text from Carla Lazzareschi and James F. Peltz, "Fewer Jobs Likely to Be Lost in Quake Than From Riots," Los Angeles Times, *21 January 1994, page 1, column 5.*

poor who eke out a daily living in often inhumane conditions in the Los Angeles basin barely merits a comment in the local newspapers, but the danger of damage to the homes of the rich and powerful summon international media orgies of truly mammoth proportions. Whether human or natural resources are at issue, Los Angeles owes its existence to reckless exploitation, breathtaking both in its scope and its indifference to the rupture of a manifold and delicate web of relationships. And a disproportionate share of the population bears the costs of sustaining the lifestyles of the few who most flagrantly defy nature.

Geologically unstable and inappropriate for the masses of humanity that crowd its topography, Los Angeles is prone to earthquakes and to a relentless cycle of fire and mud and debris slides. Privileged retreats on the flanks of hills and mountains have multiplied over the past few decades, while the shoreline has been surrounded by a ring of refineries belching pollutants into the water and air. This slow, insidious poison generated by humans only receives grudging attention from Angelenos, but the spectacular fires and devastating slides arouse armies of well-meaning volunteers to stem the revenge of nature.

And revenge it is. The work wrought by phalanxes of bulldozers ruthlessly leveling hills, woods, and stands of oak and walnut trees is systematically being undone by raging fires that billions of dollars in fire-fighting efforts are powerless to stop. When southern California's chaparral burns, it leaves a viscous residue that hastens slides. Billions of dollars more are regularly wasted in erosion and flood control and in the construction and cleaning of debris basins to contain the boulders shed by the steadily rising San Gabriel and Santa Susana mountains. Needless to say, such sums are differentially expended to protect the investments of wealthy Angelenos who choose to live in spectacular hillside homes remote from the problems of urban living. It is no small irony that even the poor pay a disproportionate share of the taxes that support the reckless living habits of those who dwell in ecologically dangerous areas.

The response to the three natural disasters compared with the uprising could not have differed more. During the November 1993 Malibu fires, millions of Angelenos went about their lives, even while watching the angry clouds of black smoke and the dancing border of the front consume thousands of acres of land and housing. Likewise when the slides came in February, Angelenos gathered around their television sets watched in fascination as entire hillsides slid into the ocean, carrying houses and cars with them. Where the earthquake did not cause serious property damage it, at a minimum, led to power outages, tainted water, choked telephone lines, and scarce resources. Stores that could open did so in attempts to maintain a semblance of order through the rationing of goods and limited access.

Perhaps nothing earned such an outpouring of local, state, national, and international aid as the 17 January 1994 earthquake. The thousands left homeless or in severely damaged dwellings, even those improvident enough not to have earthquake insurance, found the full force of the national government behind loans, grants, temporary shelter, and other necessities. Floating bond issues, raising taxes temporarily, and enacting other fiscal moves guaranteed assistance to those in need.

How different the response to these disasters than to the uprising of April 1992, which cast a pall of smoke and fear over the entire basin far beyond the responses to the other disasters. Many fled the city, others planned to follow, and most stayed locked in their homes, often guarding their property with guns. People immediately began to horde, working their way through menacing police lines or following the heavily armed National Guard patrolling corner mini-malls. Stores closed early, if they opened at all; shopping malls were deserted; and even movie theaters closed down. The racial, ethnic, and economic divisions suddenly could not be avoided. Elevated freeways no longer separated them from us, and there was little shield from the violence, or the potential for violence.

Fed by high unemployment, poor housing, limited access to basic services, and simmering resentment about unequal justice, thousands of Angelenos joined in a destructive frenzy after the Rodney King verdicts. Three years later, few of the promises of jobs, assistance, and training have been realized. Recalcitrant federal and state governments have only reluctantly dribbled out bits and pieces of aid. Grand promises to rebuild L.A. have come to nothing, even while more and more jobs disappear in the wake of industrial restructuring. The victims of the 1992 uprising found themselves, instead of treated with the outpourings of sympathy and assistance that characterized the other L.A. disasters, criminalized, blamed for their own troubles, feared and resented by much of the city, and largely ignored.

Officials and agencies found that in-your-face nature summoned much less equivocal responses than did the rage and frustration of oppressed minorities. The aftermath of all of the disasters rendered this more than clear. Looting a store turned out to merit a jail sentence and a stiff fine after the uprising, but store's price gouging of their customers ultimately merited only a small fine. Bond issues, federal loans, disaster grants, housing assistance, and other benefits flowed from all levels of government after the natural disasters, but none after the uprising. The reasoning seems to be that participants and victims in the uprising were somehow responsible for what happened to them, but no one caused the natural disasters. But in fact the damage from the fires and from the slides are directly attributable to fundamentally flawed building guidelines and zoning, and from the earthquake to construction that is often substandard. Failure to pay for earthquake insurance was also excused; federal and state agencies provided long-term, low-interest loans. Beyond this, however, a disproportionate share of tax revenues, insurance premiums, and disaster relief goes to service the precariously balanced streets and houses of fewer than 75,000 hillside homeowners.

In the meantime, the poor are criminalized and left bereft of sufficient aid to recover from the multiple swords of Damocles —unemployment, substandard health care, selective targeting by police because of race, seriously deficient schools, and lack of resources to provide alternatives to gangs that have fallen on them in the past two decades. Ronald Reagan's trickle down of wealth pooled right in the laps of the top 10% income level, leaving the other 90% a good deal poorer than they were before 1980. The only answers that Los Angeles Mayor Richard Riordan and California Governor Pete Wilson have are more police and more repression.

But outbursts of destructive fury, such as fires, slides, and earthquakes, cannot simply be contained by controlled burning, debris basins, or other stop-gap measures. Only when hillside construction is banned altogether, when hillside homeowners pay fire assessments to pay for their own disasters, and when serious building codes are developed and enforced will Los Angeles be protected from costly disasters. Likewise, human outbursts such as the 1992 uprising cannot be contained by provisional measures of oppression and criminalization; they demand substantive reform in labor laws, in education, in resource allocation, and in a system of justice that is far from color blind.

Diane Ghirardo is an architect and a professor at the School of Architecture at the University of Southern California.

Things Generally Wrong in the Universe

Herbert Muschamp

A bomb explodes, a building quakes, a cloud hangs over the horizon. Though the smoke soon disperses, public attention lingers, as if the explosion at the World Trade Center had released an important piece of information that could be discerned by turning into the rippling waves of its aftershock. The message the public is straining to hear is not reported on the evening news. It is not a matter of whodunit, howdunit, whydunit. Even after the authorities have identified suspects, interpreted motives, and recommended strategies to prevent a repeat occurrence, something intangible remains: a mood, an atmosphere that persists like background radiation.

Chaos. Turbulence on a global scale. A feeling Virginia Woolf once described in her diary as "things generally wrong in the universe." That is part of the message that came pulsing out of the World Trade Center's blasted sub-basements. And it is a message that buildings have been transmitting quite a lot lately. Dubrovnik. Sarajevo. South-Central Los Angeles. Waco.

These images of exploding buildings provoke ambivalent reactions. We respond to them with feelings of horror, anger, or fear. We identify them as problems for which there must be solutions. Suspected terrorists must be deported. Cease-fires must be negotiated. Relief should be expedited. Metal detectors

Newark, New Jersey

and surveillance cameras should be monitored with greater vigilance. Send in the National Guard.

Yet there is a sense in which these disasters are not problems. They are solutions. They provide a quick, dramatic answer to a question of agonizing complexity. What is the new world order? What is the glue that holds things together now that the global framework of the cold war has been dismantled?

Buildings mark boundaries. Individually, or in groups, they divide space into ordered regions—islands of homogeneity floating in a heterogeneous sea. The end of the cold war has subjected such boundaries to intensified pressure. For four decades, global tensions were focused on one principal boundary: the border between East and West and the difference in world outlook for which it stood. The collapse of that border has not eliminated the tension. It has only removed the focus, allowing the pressure to be dispersed elsewhere. Though Checkpoint Charlie is a thing of the past, there are now countless boundaries requiring checkpoint charlies. Religious cults. Ethnic enclaves. Corporate parks. Even the single-family suburban house. But who is the enemy for whom they are checking?

The collapse of the Berlin Wall ended an era, but it also began one. It started a process of global reordering that feels more like an unraveling. When we peer out from whatever bubble of security we occupy—a job, a walled condominium compound, the Psychic Friends Network—it is hard to discern any connective tissue between the bubbles.

Chaos is a substitute for the connective tissue. It is not the most comforting kind of order we could imagine. Still, there is comfort in the perception that we are all in this chaos together. Though the world has become fragmented, we are all fragmented equally. A community of chaos is still a community, of a kind.

Exploding buildings are this community's landmarks—its inverted arches of triumph, its sinister Taj Mahal's. They provide images of a collective experience that is otherwise elusive. Traditionally, we look to buildings to provide symbols of social cohesion. Exploding buildings now perform an equivalent symbolic role. People may build in different styles, but explosions are universal. Though each may have a different cause, they become linked in our perceptions to some fearful grand design. They focus public attention. They fill up TV screens. The World Trade Center bombing spawned a new style of disaster T-shirt.

While images of exploding buildings easily lend themselves to millennial foreboding, they should also remind us that throughout history architecture has been as much a military as a civil art. Today we deplore the fragmentation of cities into fortress enclaves. But enclave-making has always been fundamental to urban form. "A city without walls is not a city," J. F. Sobry wrote in 1776. Not long ago, Paris and Vienna were still encircled by military fortifications, and in the modern city, pleasure and the picturesque remained fused with strategic defense. In Paris, Baron Haussmann draped a facade of theaters, cafes, and shops over boulevards laid out for the benefits of troops who might be called upon to quell civil disturbances. Today it is the informational highway—with its data banks and video monitors, its surveillance cameras greeting us at every doorway—that seeks to keep the peace.

Perhaps it will take chaos theory to make sense of the complex evolving order of the post-cold-war world: its turbulence, its convoluted borders, its interacting global systems. But anyone who walks down the streets of an American inner city can get a pretty good idea of the new world order. The mix of uses and populations, the porous borders surrounding neighborhoods, the interdependency of skills and services: the city is the most accessible model we have for understanding the shape of the world after the collapse of global bipolarity.

For more than a century, in fact, our most influential urban theorists have been theorists of chaos: thinkers who have looked for order and meaning beneath the apparent chaos of urban development. Camillo Sitte, the nineteenth-century Austrian who helped found modern town planning, based his theories on the discovery that the picturesque irregularities of the medieval city were not just the result of chance but of an emerging social order. More recently, the American urbanist Kevin Lynch advocated individual perceptions as the basis of centralized planning. Thirty years ago, Jane Jacobs shook up the field of city planning by arguing passionately against the imposition of superficial visual order upon complex urban diversity. "To see complex systems of functional order as order and not chaos, takes understanding," Jacobs wrote. "The leaves dropping from the trees in the autumn, the interior of an airplane engine, the entrails of a dissected rabbit, the city desk of a newspaper, all appear to be chaos if they are seen without comprehension. Once they are understood as systems of order, they actually *look* different." (Jane Jacobs. *The Death and Life of Great American Cities* [New York: Random House, 1961])

These urban theorists have not been advocating anarchy. On the contrary, each of them sought to identify urban forms appropriate to modern democracy and to define the role of government in the shaping of those forms. The environmentalist Jean Gardner observes that what we often perceive as disorder is simply a sign of social inclusiveness—people are participating. Sitte valued the irregular design of medieval city squares because they represented the social rise of the craft guilds. Jacobs extolled the New York City street as a self-policing entity, secured by "eyes on the street"—people drawn by the linkage of heterogeneous uses.

The end of the cold-war years has renewed the urgency of these ideas, for cities were among the casualties of those years. Private enterprise became synonymous with public good; the public sphere abdicated its responsibility to steer private interest toward the public good. But inner cities are now the laboratories for change. They are microcosms of a new world order—places where the conflict between heterogeneity and homogeneity is being staged in the glare of television.

The chaos that erupted in 1992 in South-Central Los Angeles was caused in large part by the lack of integration between the homogenized culture of corporations and developers and the culture of minority neighborhoods. And now it is widely reported that efforts to "rebuild L.A." have failed. But what did people expect to happen in a year's time? For that matter, what do they expect now? Do inner-city neighborhoods want to be remade in the image of corporate culture? Must success always look like a Marriott Hotel? A Kmart? A cluster of glass high rises? Or are we prepared to acknowledge that, for integration to occur, the corporate culture must also be remade?

Not readily. It is easier to imagine blowing things sky high than to give up homogenized order as a measure of urban success. It is easier to talk about the breakup of the former Soviet Union than to reintegrate our own fragmented society, particularly since reintegration requires the breakup of our own cold-war apparatus. Heterogeneity, by definition, presupposes the foreign, the unknown—the terrorist explosion, the decline of the West, the vision of "things generally wrong in the universe"—than to overcome that fear. Breaking up is hard to do. Rethinking how to build is harder.

This text is an edited version of "Things Generally Wrong In the Universe," originally published in New York Times, *30 May 1993, 30H.*

Herbert Muschamp is the architecture critic of New York Times.

Afterworlds

Kyong Park

Through the realization of nuclear power, we have crossed the threshold where future and past are no longer comfortably aligned, but out of order. By disrupting the eternal significance of stabilized particle matters into a split second of enormous discontent, we have placed life in a vacuum that defies the progression of time and evolution. Both the linearity and articulation of culture are endangered in this age of energy and information, where our bodies, minds, identities, sexuality, and even language are digitally interchangeable or radically metamorphic.

Like a genie let loose from the innermost core of a nuclear reactor, the end of the cold war has unleashed regional and civic conflicts worldwide. By reinterpreting the national, ethnic, and religious boundaries that were instituted by the victors of World War II, contemporary global affairs have returned to the geopolitical markings of a half century ago. The defenders of Sarajevo and Grozny, dressed in domestic and hunting attires, like the Korean-American storekeepers protecting their businesses during the Los Angeles riots, suggest the deconstruction of advanced military warfare. 1995 is 1945.

The return of force to the populace through urban gangs, drug and weapon trafficking, and international terrorism has downscaled a globally envisioned war to the intimacy of individual and communal power. This raises the deadening thought

New York City

that distinctions between civilian and military have been lost and that the miniaturization of war into urban theaters can subject any city and any architecture to military operations. Sarajevo, Grozny, Mogadishu, Baghdad, Port-au-Prince, Gaza City, and Hebron are the marquees of this new and decentralized war. As cultural documents these cities and their architectures are being slowly erased. Cities have themselves become mortal.

Kyong Park is the founder and director of StoreFront for Art and Architecture.

StoreFront for Art and Architecture is a not-for-profit organization established in 1982. StoreFront's programs are supported by: The Andy Warhol Foundation for the Visual Arts, Inc., The Greenwall Foundation, The Jerome Foundation, The J. M. Kaplan Fund, The Graham Foundation for Advanced Studies in the Fine Arts, The LEF Foundation, The Joyce Mertz Gilmore Foundation, The Reed Foundation, The Rockefeller Foundation, The National Endowment for the Arts, The New York State Council on the Arts, The New York City Department of Cultural Affairs, and individual contributors.

StoreFront Books is dedicated to the exploration and mapping of new world disorder and its architecture. A continuation and expansion of our previous publications, *Reports* and *Front*, this new series will provide documentation and commentary relating to StoreFront exhibitions and other programs. StoreFront Books reflects a cultural mosaic of issues concerning the environment, technology, ecology, and aesthetics. Along with upcoming volumes that include *Eco-Tec*, *Queer Space*, *The Suburban Discipline*, and *Refugee City*, *Mortal City* presents StoreFront for Art and Architecture as a living proof of cultural resistance.

StoreFront for Art and Architecture
97 Kenmare Street, New York, NY 10012
Tel: 212.431.5795 Fax: 212.431 5755